EBURY PRESS
MUNGER KI RANI

Manisha Rani is one of India's most popular digital creators. A finalist on the reality show *Bigg Boss OTT 2* and a celebrated performer on *Jhalak Dikhhla Jaa*, Manisha continues to break barriers and redefine what success looks like for the new generation. *Munger ki Rani* is her first book.

Sakett Saawhney has spent over twenty-five years in media production, during which he founded the talent agency People Like US and managed top talent. He has produced acclaimed projects such as *Zanjeer* and *Escaype Live*, earning multiple awards.

Munger ki Rani

From Bihar's Heartland to a Billion Hearts

MANISHA RANI
as told to SAKETT SAAWHNEY

An imprint of Penguin Random House

EBURY PRESS

Ebury Press is an imprint of the Penguin Random House group of companies whose addresses can be found at global.penguinrandomhouse.com

Published by Penguin Random House India Pvt. Ltd
4th Floor, Capital Tower 1, MG Road,
Gurugram 122 002, Haryana, India

First published in Ebury Press by Penguin Random House India 2025

Copyright © Manisha Rani and Sakett Saawhney 2025

All rights reserved

10 9 8 7 6 5 4 3 2 1

The views and opinions expressed in this book are the authors' own and the facts are as reported by them which have been verified to the extent possible, and the publishers are not in any way liable for the same.

Please note that no part of this book may be used or reproduced in any manner for the purpose of training artificial intelligence technologies or systems.

ISBN 9780143475507

Typeset in Bembo Std by Manipal Technologies Limited, Manipal
Printed and bound in India by Replika Press Pvt. Ltd.

This book is sold subject to the condition that it shall not, by way of trade or otherwise, be lent, resold, hired out or otherwise circulated without the publisher's prior consent in any form of binding or cover other than that in which it is published and without a similar condition including this condition being imposed on the subsequent purchaser.

www.penguin.co.in

For my mother, late Asha Sawhney—your love and strength continue to guide me every day. This book is for you.

Contents

Introduction ix

1. The Cursed Blessing 1
2. Madhavi, Meera or Manisha? 21
3. Survival Amidst Separation 41
4. A Daughter's Choice 61
5. Determined to Achieve 77
6. The Letter Under the Pillow 87
7. Undeterred: Facing Unknown Obstacles with Courage 97
8. Mumbai: The City of Dreams 107
9. The Breakthrough 119
10. Ek Bihari Sab Par Bhari 135

Acknowledgements 155

Introduction

From the dusty lanes of Munger, a town nestled in the heart of Bihar, a dream took flight, embodied in a spirited young girl named Manisha. Stories echo through the village, tales of her skilled performances that painted vivid pictures against the backdrop of the humble lives of the villagers. Growing up amidst cultural richness but economic hardship, Manisha found solace and escape in the performing arts, her imagination blossoming like a lotus in a murky pond. She fought against the societal norms and resource constraints that threatened to clip her wings, yet her resolve burned brighter with each passing day. Her spirit, fuelled by the steady support of her family and friends, propelled her forward, drawing the attention of local artists who recognized the spark within her. Regional dance competitions became her stage, each performance proving her dedication. With each acclamation, the world seemed to widen, beckoning her towards the dazzling realm of entertainment.

Manisha Rani's arrival in my professional sphere was initiated by a serendipitous phone call from Rohini, a dear friend and a media lawyer by profession. 'Sakett,' she began, her voice brimming with enthusiasm, 'I was at a café, and I met this girl, Manisha Rani. She's a TikToker and is on Instagram, apparently quite popular, and she's been chosen for *Bigg Boss OTT* Season Two. She's searching for a dependable agent, and you were the first person who came to my mind. I think you two would be a good fit. Give her a call.' My friend was aware that I had recently launched a boutique agency that aimed at representing emerging talents, those rising stars often overlooked by larger agencies. I had noticed a gap in the market, a need for guidance among TikTokers, influencers and aspiring actors who often find themselves adrift after experiencing initial success. They require proper representation and management to advance their careers effectively. Before this unexpected recommendation, I had only a fleeting impression of Manisha Rani. I recalled seeing her on an episode of *The Kapil Sharma Show*, where she had spontaneously composed a couplet, a feat that struck me as genuinely impressive. Beyond that, I was in the dark about her story, her background or the extent of her fame on TikTok.

I decided to delve into the possibilities that Rohini had presented and, with a sense of cautious optimism, dialled the number she'd provided. A young male voice answered on the other end, introducing himself as Vishal, a friend of Manisha. I introduced myself and explained that Rohini had suggested I contact them. To my surprise, the very next morning, Vishal and Manisha were sitting across from me in my office. We all know that viral sensations on platforms like TikTok and Instagram often experience fleeting fame: their success quickly fades due to the notoriously short attention spans of online viewers. However, Manisha was different—she was holding her own, boasting an impressive four million followers on Instagram and around 3,00,000 on TikTok before the latter was banned in India. From the moment our meeting began, I felt a connection, a sense that we could forge a successful path together. She struck me as genuine, diligent and undeniably charming. She proudly showcased her vlogs and other work on YouTube, where she already had a substantial following of around 3,00,000 subscribers. Impressed by her talent and potential, I offered her an exclusive contract for three years, a decision I felt would be mutually beneficial. Then, just two weeks later, she embarked on a new adventure, stepping into the spotlight of the *Bigg Boss* house, ready to face whatever challenges awaited her there.

What drew me to her initially was a spark, a certain '*zid*', as they say, that I could see in her eyes. I remember our first conversation vividly; she approached me, a mix of eagerness and apprehension in her voice, addressing me as '*bhaiya*'. Her question, 'You've already been through this; will you give me some tips on how to survive?', struck a chord with me. Of course, there were no foolproof tips for navigating the unscripted chaos that awaited her.

I could only offer a glimpse into the inner workings of the show, how it might play games with her mind and the various trials she would face and emotions she would feel. I painted an honest picture, hoping to prepare her for the storm ahead. Her response, 'You just hold fort outside. I'll be a finalist, and I'll come out and see you,' was both endearing and audacious. In that moment, she was just a young, loveable girl, making a bold declaration that seemed almost too big for her. I couldn't help but be amused, thinking, 'Let's see if she can actually pull it off.' And, to my surprise and admiration, she did. She emerged from the crucible of the show, not unscathed, but undeniably a finalist, having proven her mettle against the odds.

Manisha's genuine nature, the very essence of who she was remained untainted, a beacon shining brightly for the world to witness. Whatever her journey inside the *Bigg Boss* house entailed during those intense six weeks, she emerged bruised, but with her core values intact, and this spoke volumes about the integrity of her character. There were no affected airs and graces, no calculated performances for the cameras, absolutely nothing even remotely scripted about her demeanor; she was and remains an authentic talent, radiating a gracious aura and honest nature that resolutely shone through the manufactured drama and orchestrated conflicts. Manisha never succumbed to the temptation of pretending to be somebody she wasn't; instead, she decided to express her raw and authentic self, allowing the world to glimpse the woman she is in her everyday life.

Victory can sometimes be found outside the conventional definitions of winning. She may not have won the trophy, but she emerged with something perhaps far more enduring: the unwavering adoration and support of millions. A digital army numbering eleven million rallied behind her on Instagram, their hearts captured by her journey, her spirit, her authentic self. Introduced simply as a contestant from Munger she was quickly embraced as something more—'Bihar ki Rani', a queen of hearts, for an entire region. That title, bestowed by the people, speaks volumes, echoing louder than any official crown. It speaks of connection, of a legacy built not on fleeting triumph, but on genuine impact.

During the six weeks that Manisha graced the *Bigg Boss* studio house, I found myself drawn into the orbit of her life. Meeting her father, her sister and her best friend Vishal, each interaction peeled back another layer of her experiences. I was struck by her unwavering grit, which seemed to emanate from her very core. It was this indomitable spirit that made me to want to share her story, to narrate the journey of a remarkable young woman. This wasn't just about fleeting fame; it was about the relentless pursuit of a dream, the commitment to achieving what she had set her heart on. Manisha's story transcended the ordinary; it gave hope to anyone who dared to dream beyond their circumstances. Even after the applause of *Bigg Boss* died, Manisha refused to let her ambition wane. The dancer within her yearned for a new stage, a new challenge: *Jhalak Dikhhla Jaa*. 'Bhaiya, I want to do this show,' she declared, her eyes shining with a now-familiar spark. But the path wasn't straightforward, because of initial resistance from the channel and a preference for established names over influencers. Yet, Manisha remained resolute.

Jhalak Dikhhla Jaa's Season 11 shimmered with an almost blinding array of talent, a testament to the artistic spirit that courses through our nation. Each contestant, a brush stroke on the canvas of the competition, contributed to a masterpiece of movement and emotion. And then came the wild cards, a surge of fresh hues on this canvas. Awez Darbar, Sagar Parekh, Dhanashree Verma, Nikhita Gandhi, Glenn Saldanha—each name held a promise of untold stories waiting to be told through the language of dance. And then, Manisha Rani, a name that resonated differently. She was facing off against seasoned performers, individuals who had dedicated years to honing their craft. The weight of expectation was palpable, amplified by the fact that only four of the wild card entrants would advance. Armed with raw talent and infectious enthusiasm, she was stepping into an arena dominated by technical prowess, a world where she was about to rewrite the rules.

After seeing her in *Bigg Boss*, I had confidence that Manisha would pour her heart and soul into whatever endeavour she chose. In the ten-season history of *Jhalak*

Dikhhla Jaa, no wild card contestant had ever claimed the coveted trophy. It felt like a unique destiny that awaited Manisha, a narrative yet unwritten, but one I secretly hoped she would rewrite. I remember, clear as day, the conversation we had before she decided to enter. I had advised her with the sincerity of a brother, urging her to wait, to sit out Season 11, and put the time into practising and honing her dancing skills, with the aim of entering Season 12 fully prepared. We sat together, me trying to impart every ounce of belief I had in her, fully convinced that she possessed the potential to excel, yet also fearing that her lack of formal dance training would ultimately hold her back from reaching the very top. I told her that the steep odds of a wild card entry winning the trophy. Her disarming simple response still echoes in my mind: 'Bhaiya, please get me a wild card entry for this; what hasn't been done till today, Manisha Rani will do.' And she did; Manisha was the first wild card contestant in the history of *Jhalak Dikhhla Jaa* who actually won the trophy.

It was this serene confidence, which seemed to emanate from her very being, that sparked the initial embers of inspiration for this book. Observing this faith in her own potential, even amidst challenges, made me realize the power of self-assurance. It's my sincere hope that readers of this narrative will also find themselves ignited by that same spark and emboldened to embrace their aspirations, no matter how grand they may seem. To dream big is one thing, but belief is the crucial catalyst in

Introduction

transforming those dreams into tangible realities. Manisha Rani possesses a rare and radiant talent, a unique blend of creativity, resoluteness and authenticity that sets her apart. To have even a small role in documenting and sharing her story is an immense honour, a privilege that I hold with deep gratitude and respect.

1

The Cursed Blessing

1

The Cursed Blessing

'*Phir se ladki*!?' (Again another girl!?)

I was born in a village nestled in the rural district of Munger, Bihar, India, where age-old traditions and patriarchal conventions still reign supreme, and the birth of a daughter is generally welcomed with resignation. Slow-paced development, if any happens, has little impact on people's lifestyles there. But in one poor home, a new story began to unfold—one of hope, defiance and the relentless pursuit of progress.

I am from a culture in which the birth of a girl is viewed as a financial burden. My parents, Ragini and Manoj, or Maa or Baba as I call them, already had a daughter. In a town where the community valued sons over daughters, the birth of another daughter was interpreted as a kind of curse. However, from the moment I was born my parents saw me as a beacon of light, a blessing in disguise. My mother recounts that when she cradled me in her arms after birth, she murmured to my father, 'Our little Lakshmi has come to bless us,' and Baba affectionately added, 'She is our joy, not our burden.' However, the town elders, mired in tradition, were not as welcoming. The whispers began almost immediately, as people speculated about my family's future and the weight of the dowry obligations that my father would have to undertake. '*Yeh to dahej nahi de payega,*' (He won't be able to afford her dowry) was their verdict.

But Munger's archaic habits did not overshadow my youth. Despite the murmurs and social pressure, Maa and Baba made a daring decision. They would provide me with formal educational opportunities and other possibilities that were mostly denied to girls in our community. They believed that a girl deserved to pursue her full potential, regardless of cultural expectations. My father was firm: 'Our daughters will be educated. They will have options.' Growing up, my mother constantly encouraged me, 'You will learn, grow and choose your own path.' As the years went by, the townsfolk watched all that went on in our family with a mix of curiosity and disapproval. While most girls my age were pulled out of school and prepared for early marriage, I continued my studies. My parents' determination set them apart, making them a source of inspiration to some, but gossip to most.

'She's almost thirteen. Why isn't she being prepared for marriage?' asked one elder sceptically.

'Education won't help her in the kitchen,' another scoffed.

Baghi aur Baghavat: The Rebel and the Rebellion

I thrived in school. My curiosity knew no bounds, and from very early on, I dreamt of a world beyond the confines of Munger. My parents' firm support helped my ambitions grow, but the town elders' expectations loomed large. In Munger, a girl's destiny was often sealed by tradition and societal norms. As I approached my fourteenth birthday, the pressure really started to ramp up. I recall that almost everyone seemed to want me married off. You see, in my village, turning fourteen is a big deal—it's when a lot of girls get married off, and their futures are decided by generational practices instead of what they wished for. People in the town began to question my parents going against tradition and choosing to keep me in school: '*Ladki ki shadi nahi karni hai kya? Samaaj mein naak katvaoge kya?*' (Aren't you going to get the girl married? Do you want to be shamed by society?)

'Why waste money on education? She'll just get married,' another judgemental neighbour questioned.

Yet, my parents remained calm and composed. They were willing to face isolation, whispers and even outright disapproval for the sake of their daughter's future. They believed in my potential and desired to give me a chance to pursue my dreams, no matter the cost.

'Manisha deserves more than this town can offer. She deserves to choose,' Maa asserted fiercely.

'We will stand by her, against all odds,' Baba added, resolute.

As I continued my studies, I became more and more aware of the sacrifices my parents were making. Their quiet rebellion against the deeply entrenched mores of Munger was both inspiring and a bit scary. I realized that my future was this delicate balance between my dreams and the harsh realities of our world.

The Ultimate Challenge

One evening, as the family sat together, a knock on the door shattered the calm. Some elders belonging to our community entered, accompanied by a potential groom's family. The proposal was unexpected, and the elders made it clear that the time had come for me to follow the traditional path.

'It's time, Manoj. Manisha is of age. The boy's family is respectable. This is the best match we can find,' one of the elders stated gravely to my father.

My parents exchanged a glance, their faces reflecting a mix of fear and resolve. They had hoped for more time, but now they faced the ultimate test of their convictions. The elders waited for an answer, the weight of tradition hanging heavy in the room.

'We appreciate your concern, but Manisha is still studying. We believe she has a bright future ahead,' Baba responded calmly but firmly.

The elders frowned, and their expressions hardened. The atmosphere grew tense as the village's rigid expectations clashed with the family's progressive beliefs. The room felt stifling, the silence thick with unspoken words.

'Think carefully, Manoj. This is the last good offer she might get. You know what the village will say if you refuse,' warned one elder.

The moment hung in the air, a pivotal decision between tradition and change. Would my parents stand firm in their resolve, risking the scorn of the entire village? Or would they bow to the pressures of their community, ensuring my future was one of conformity?

As the oil lamp flickered, casting shadows on the walls, I looked at my parents with a pounding heart. The decision before them would shape the course of my life. It remained suspended in the stillness of the night, a cliffhanger that left me—and the future of my family—dangling in the balance. My parents passed an uneasy and sleepless night immersed in their past and thinking about their future. The dawn of a new day would bring clarity and relief, but for now, the fate of my dreams remained uncertain, wrapped in the shadows of tradition.

My Fortress

Munger is known for its historical heritage and forts. The famous fort of Mir Qasim, the last nawab of Bengal, situated on the banks of the Ganges, attracts people from all over the world. However, the neighbourhood I was born in was a collection of kutcha houses where people still needed to go out of the town for their daily needs. If someone wanted to do something big in life, they had to move out of Munger and settle in big cities. But no one had any idea that this region was about to see a revolution that would set Munger on Bihar's map in golden letters. And every gust of wind in Munger's streets would reach each girl, urging her to dream big and achieve great things in her life.

Amidst Munger's narrow streets, there stood another brick-and-mortar fort against social norms, where four brothers and two sisters lived with their parents, a family looking for a match for one of their sons to marry. No one understood what twists and turns this story would take or under what conditions it would unfold. However, in Jamalpur, just eight kilometres away from Munger, instead of stepping into the ninth grade in school, a fourteen-year-old girl, Ragini, my mother, became a bride.

Child marriage has been a deep-rooted practice in India, often driven by societal pressures and customs that prioritize the safety and honour of daughters over their education and personal aspirations. In many communities, marrying off girls young is seen as a protective measure against threats, leading families to make life-altering decisions for their children. This cultural norm not only curtails the childhood of many girls but also significantly impacts their future prospects.

The story of my parents illustrates the harsh realities faced by countless young brides. As Ragini left her childhood home, her heart was filled with conflicting emotions—excitement for a new life and sorrow for the dreams she had to abandon. Despite having just completed her eighth grade exams, the weight of her new responsibilities ended her hopes for continued education. The veil that adorned her face symbolized the expectations of modesty and obedience and marked a swift transition from girlhood to womanhood that many girls experience in silence.

My mother recounts that as soon as she walked inside her husband's house, her senses were assaulted by a barrage of sounds and smells. The thatched roof, fashioned from field straw, echoed the beat of rainfall, which provided the only respite from the sweltering humidity. A modest hearth, constantly blazing with the flames of cooking pots, offered nutrition for the family gathered around it. It was here that she was expected to fulfil her duties as a wife, a daughter-in-law and, eventually, a mother. Every corner of the house seemed to whisper tales of generations past, of women who had lived there, their footsteps softened by the weight of patriarchal norms and expectation.

Maa did her best to observe and absorb all that was happening around her. As she sat on a chair in the veranda with her sisters-in-law, she could see people moving around her through the clouded vision of her semi-transparent *ghoonghat*. Amazed at all the activity around her, she kept wondering what would happen next, as others carried chairs from one area of the house to another and arranged them, as if someone was ready to arrive and perform some rite. The ladies of the house were busy preparing snacks and tea for arriving guests. In the background she could hear children screaming out at each other in funny tones in a neighbouring house. They were playing '*Bhootni Bhawani tera ghar konsa*' (a local game where one player gives a task to other players of a particular spot to be touched, without being tapped by that one player who gave the task). Just a week earlier, she had been playing the same game with her friends and cousins in Jamalpur. This was already fading into memory.

Maa felt hesitant and shy to use the washroom because she was too intimidated by the unfamiliar sights and sounds. Who would direct her to the washroom? How she would she be able to manage anything with such heavy attire on? She could not slip into something more comfortable until given permission. With all the chaos around her, asking for help to use the restroom felt like requesting a truce in combat. Would anyone listen to her? Gathering all her courage, she searched for the most familiar face nearby while she sat in the veranda and finally caught the attention of one of her sisters-in-law, Seema, 'Seema didi, I need to go to the washroom,'

Ragini whispered urgently. Seema, herself very busy packing sweets in small paper pouches, started searching for her elder sister to assist the new bride, but Ragini insisted Seema help her and not call anyone else. Sensing the shyness and discomfort Ragini was facing, Seema kept her work aside and said, '*Chalo Bhabhi*' (Let's go).

My mother recounts that as she approached the washroom, the sight of withered flowers scattered around the house evoked a deep sense of loss. These flowers, once full of life, now lay forgotten, much like Ragini's own dreams. She wondered about the unknowns of her new life after marriage: how she would adapt to her surroundings and find happiness in a world that felt so foreign? The stark contrast between the wilted flowers and the small marigold buds in a nearby pot reminded her of her past and her hopes for a blossoming future.

In that moment, Maa's thoughts were interrupted by Seema, who gently inquired about her well-being. This brief exchange brought Maa back to reality. She realized that just like the marigold buds waiting for the right moment to bloom, she too had the potential to grow and thrive in her new environment. The journey ahead was uncertain, but it was filled with possibilities waiting for her.

Amidst these joyous marriage celebrations, Ragini found herself overcome with a strong sense of disconnection. Having spent most of her time within the confines of the ghoonghat, she was unable to truly engage with the people surrounding her. Instead of faces, she had come to recognize the guests by their feet and voices, she felt confused by this and the bustling atmosphere around her. My mother's memory highlights the often-overlooked emotional turmoil that can accompany traditional marriage rituals. As she relied on the sound of voices and the sight of feet to identify those around her, the warmth and intimacy of personal connections became obscured, and she felt isolated. The washroom, a mundane yet necessary space, was a poignant symbol of her discomfort and hesitation in this unfamiliar environment.

As Seema led my mother back to the veranda, she told her about the various relatives and neighbours there and guided her about what and what not to speak with specific relatives with whom they didn't share good bonds. All the while, my mother kept wondering why the house was such a beehive of activity. It was because an important ritual known as '*munh dikhayi*' or the 'face reveal' was about begin. This is a traditional ceremony in which the bride is introduced to the groom's family for the first time after the wedding. During the ceremony, a woman, usually the bride's mother-in-law, reveals the bride's face and showers her with gifts as a sign of welcome. My mother, just a child herself, had no idea about this tradition. It was noon, when people started coming in the veranda and settled into the chairs opposite a throne-like seating arrangement. 'Ragini, you have to sit there,' Baba murmured. He had been standing behind the chair she had been sitting on for the past two hours. Ragini recognized his voice but couldn't see which direction he was pointing towards. Confused and perhaps a bit dehydrated because she dare not ask for much water for the fear of going to the washroom, she tried to gather her words to ask him to repeat where she should sit. Before she could speak, Seema came up to her and said, '*Chalo Bhabhi*, (Let's go, Bhabhi). I will tell you where to sit.'

My mother recalls that she had never attended such a ceremony before her own, because it was mostly for adults. The moment arrived when Manoj's mother lifted the ghoonghat and said, 'My beautiful daughter-in-law, may no evil eye befall her. Daughter, may your marital life be blessed, stay happy.' She ended by giving her a warm side hug and left Rs 20 as a token of blessing in her lap. The queue moved forward—one by one, the ladies from the neighbourhood and close relatives of Manoj from Munger came in and lifted the ghoonghat. They left their blessings in her lap just like her mother-in-law did. This was the first time she could see the new faces around her, and she glanced quickly and often around the unfamiliar surroundings.

Ragini felt as if she were a product being reviewed in the marketplace, with others passing judgement. She could hear a conversation from the periphery about how small her feet were. She was now very uncomfortable and wanted to get out of the spotlight. However, she managed to stick around until the end, after everyone else had left. By now, my mother had accepted her fate and begun to believe that this was her new life, one to which she needed to adjust and learn to live in comfortably, even though she had many doubts about the future, her incomplete studies and various responsibilities she would be saddled with once this wedding was finally over.

Among these myriad issues, one thing concerned her the most. Maa had no prior experience wearing a ghoonghat; she may have covered her head in religious places or while worshipping, but she had no idea how uncomfortable a permanent ghoonghat might be for a newlywed lady. Behind the veil, she dreamt of a future in which her voice would be heard, and her desires would take flight. Ragini had always wanted to study well and earn herself a name through education, but she hadn't gathered the courage to contest the decisions made by the elders of the house yet. This was the reason why Ragini's marriage was arranged at such a young age, and at that time, she didn't consider it a big deal. However, Maa was secretly worried about completing the rest of her studies. Outside the confines of her ghoonghat, the world appeared vast and unknowable, a labyrinth of possibilities and also pitfalls. However, she couldn't abandon the centuries-old tradition, even though she wasn't even old enough to properly drape a sari. She had been dressed in bridal garb and taken to Munger to marry Manoj.

Although Ragini came from a poor family, her family had given Manoj's family approximately Rs 10,000 in cash as dowry at that time. This was a time when asking for dowry was not necessary; it was the bride's family itself who thought that they had to give this dowry in their daughter's marriage. And at that time, Rs 10,000 would be equivalent to almost Rs 10,00,000 today. Amidst all this, Ragini and Manoj's relationship had been formed as husband and wife.

As a new bride, life with four brothers and two sisters was initially quite enjoyable, but this was short-lived. Just three days after the wedding, all the guests who had stayed during the wedding festivities began to leave for their respective homes. The house, which had been noisy and bustling with guests and their children, had now quietened down. Ragini was now faced with the responsibility of Manoj's family—which now numbered nine people including her—a responsibility that had fallen on her shoulders at such a young age. My mother who, just two weeks ago, had been playing hide-and-seek with her friends in the streets of Jamalpur, was now expected to run the house. Every day, Ragini would wake up in the morning, clean the house and prepare breakfast for everyone. Then she would move on to other household chores—preparing lunch by noon, assisting her mother-in-law with her tasks and finally ensuring that everyone in the house had a warm meal when the men returned home in the evening. This became Ragini's life at the age of fourteen. Cooking three meals a day for the nine people in the house was no easy task. Although Seema *bhua* often lent a helping hand, hardly anyone else in the house would pitch in to assist Ragini with any chore. With each passing day, Maa learned to manage the complexities of her new role, drawing strength from the bonds of sisterhood she formed with the women in her new family.

Time passed; Maa got familiar with the rhythm of her new home and began to contemplate continuing her education. She discussed it with Baba and he supported her, saying, 'Absolutely, you should complete your education, and we have no objection to that. You can continue your studies right here.' Maa had passed her eighth grade exams in Jamalpur before getting married and moving to Munger; she was now enrolled in the ninth grade in a school nearby.

Maa now had to manage both her household duties and studies while staying at home. Continuing one's education after marriage may sound easy, but for Maa, it was a balancing act: on one side, the smoke from the *chulha* rising and the roti burning, and on the other, she would open her textbooks and notebooks, flipping through their pages intermittently. As the ninth grade examinations neared, Maa realized how difficult it was for her to study while juggling so many duties. She would often tell herself that she would not let her children be consumed by all this chaos and would instead give them the opportunity to study well, prosper academically and achieve something meaningful in life. Though Ragini couldn't pursue her own aspirations, she wanted her children to fulfil theirs and achieve anything they chose. Despite all odds, she completed her tests for the ninth, tenth, eleventh and twelfth grades. She couldn't continue studying further thereafter.

As time passed, my uncles married, and while Baba completely supported Maa's education, the household in Munger stayed unchanged, much like most of north India, where women were not allowed to wander far from home. They had to cover themselves completely whenever they went out and were expected to complete all their duties outside the house during the day and finally return home on time. Furthermore, no lady could even go to the roof of the house unless she had some work there. Women's access to the outside world was restricted; this was the norm in other families in this society too. My uncles likewise prevented their spouses and sisters from leaving the house unnecessarily. Nor were women given much opportunity to speak in front of family elders and males. It was standard practice in Munger for males to decide where the children, particularly the girls, would study, what clothes they would wear, when they would go to the roof and when they could go outdoors.

Amidst all this, Baba and Maa's perspective was evolving. They had had a son and a daughter, and the village shared in their joy. This changed when I was born. The villagers couldn't feign any special happiness at the birth of another daughter, as most of them considered daughters a burden. In simple terms, having a daughter meant that as she matured, they would face a variety of challenges; and, when she finally grew up, they would have to pay a substantial dowry for her wedding. On the other hand, having a son meant that they would receive a dowry when he married and would not have to worry about his well-being as he grew older.

However, our family was a bit different from the rest of the townspeople. Daughters were always considered precious in our home, and no distinction was made between having a son or a daughter. Whether it was a son or a daughter, the entire family celebrated, saying, 'If it's a son, he's my king, and if it's a daughter, the Goddess of Wealth has come to my home.' The family was growing, and as it did, the love among all family members grew continuously.

Growing up in a small town like Munger, I often felt like the world had predetermined expectations for me based solely on my gender. It was a common belief that girls were destined to lead lives of limited opportunities and restricted potential. However, I consider myself incredibly fortunate to have been raised in a family where sons and daughters were seen as equals, with the same opportunities and capabilities. This mindset, though simple in nature, was quite rare in my town, and it played a crucial role in shaping the person I am today. When I was a young girl, no one could have predicted the heights I would go on to reach. To the world, I appeared to be just an ordinary girl child; little did they know that I would defy all odds and emerge as a successful individual. The journey from being underestimated to being celebrated has been eventful, but one that has ultimately vindicated my resolve to break societal norms and pave my own path towards success.

2

Madhavi, Meera or Manisha?

The Joy of Arrival: A Family's Celebration

The moment I entered this world, my family was enveloped in happiness. The joyous shout of 'Lakshmi has arrived!' resonated throughout our home, heralding the beginning of my life. While there were a few outsiders who frowned upon the birth of another daughter, my family and many of our relatives embraced my arrival with open hearts, dismissing any negativity and celebrating the love and hope that I brought into their lives.

As the youngest child, I was greeted with joy by my siblings, who were excited to welcome their little sister, and this happiness radiated throughout our household. Welcoming a new baby into the family is one of life's most precious occasions. It transforms not just the household but also the hearts of everyone involved. Well-wishers flocked to meet me, eager to share in the happiness. Each visitor came bearing sweets, gifts and heartfelt blessings, all of which enriched the family's experience. The air was filled with laughter as stories were shared and memories created. As one elderly neighbour wisely noted, 'A new baby brings new blessings.' This sentiment rang true as each visit added layers of delight to an already vibrant household.

The celebration extended beyond the walls of our home. Our family was well-loved in their community. The local temple held a special prayer ceremony to bless the newborn, attended by neighbours and family friends. 'May she have a long, healthy and prosperous life,' whispered the priest as the family offered prayers and sweets.

When the time came for the naming ceremony, the family was abuzz with excitement as they gathered to discuss my name. Ragini, cradling her newborn daughter in her arms, had a serene smile on her face. She had a name in mind, one that she believed would be perfect for her little girl.

'I think we should name her Madhavi,' she suggested softly, looking down at the baby's cherubic face. 'It means unique, and I feel she's going to be someone special.'

Manoj, sitting beside her, nodded thoughtfully. 'Madhavi is a beautiful name, Ragini. But I was thinking we could name her Manisha. It means wisdom, and I hope she grows up to be wise and kind.'

My elder sister, excited to have a baby sister, chimed in with her own suggestion. 'How about we call her Rani? She's our little princess, after all!'

The room erupted in laughter. Friends and relatives added their suggestions, each name reflecting their hopes and dreams for the baby. Names like Meera, symbolizing prosperity, and Diya, meaning light, were proposed.

In the end, Manoj's suggestion resonated the most. 'Manisha Rani,' he said, combining both names. 'Wisdom and a princess. It's perfect.'

Everyone agreed, and thus I was named Manisha Rani.

As I grew up, I was surrounded by love and laughter. In many families, including mine, younger siblings often found themselves in hand-me-downs from their elder brothers and sisters. This was certainly true in my case—my wardrobe consisted of clothes that once belonged to my siblings. Sometimes, my mother dressed me in my brother's clothes, that made me look like a boy, while at other times I donned my sister's dresses. This practice is not just a quirky family tradition; it is a common experience in many households even today.

Our house was always alive with various activities. Didi became my first best friend and companion, and we brothers and sisters spent many gay hours in the courtyard, our laughter echoing through the neighbourhood. I shared a special bond with my brother, Rohit. Our playful banter and shared adventures enriched our childhood. Whether climbing trees, chasing butterflies or playing cricket in the narrow roads of Munger, our days were filled with laughter and companionship. We were inseparable; not just siblings but best friends who supported each other in everything. I often practised my dance routines with Rohit cheering me on; he sometimes even attempted to mimic my dance moves, causing us all to burst into laughter.

Maa would entertain us with folk tales and stories from Indian mythology, sparking my imagination and creativity. I was an attentive listener, and was often spellbound by these stories. I used to beg my mother to repeat one of my favourite stories, 'The Brave Princess and the Wise Sage.' Maa would indulge me and begin the tale in a soft voice,

'Once upon a time, in a distant kingdom, there lived a brave princess named Aanya. Unlike other princesses who spent their days in the palace, surrounded by luxury, Aanya was adventurous and loved exploring the vast forests and mountains around her kingdom.'

Interrupting, I asked, 'Maa, what does "sage" mean?' My mother explained, 'A wise person. Now listen to the rest of the story!'

From a young age, Aanya had been fascinated by the stories of the great sage Arnav, who lived in a cave high up in the mountains. Known for his wisdom and knowledge, many sought his guidance. One day, Aanya decided to find the sage and learn from him.

Despite the objections of her royal advisors and the concern of her parents, Aanya set off on her journey. She travelled through dense forests, crossed turbulent rivers and climbed steep mountains. Along the way, she encountered wild animals, endured harsh weather and found her own food and shelter. But Aanya was courageous, never letting fear or fatigue deter her.

Finally, after days of travel, Aanya reached the sage's cave. The sage welcomed her with a warm smile and invited her to stay. For several weeks, Aanya lived with the sage, learning about the secrets of nature, the importance of kindness and the power of knowledge. The sage taught her to meditate, find inner peace and see the world with a clear and compassionate heart.

One day, the sage told Aanya it was time for her to return to her kingdom. He gave her a small, plain-looking box and said, 'Inside this box is the greatest treasure you will ever find. Use it wisely, Princess.'

Curiosity gripped me and once again I interrupted the telling, 'Maa, what was inside the box that the sage gave to the princess?' Maa smiled and replied, 'You'll find out if you listen to the next part of the story!'

Aanya thanked the sage and made her way back home. The journey back was just as arduous, but she was now stronger and wiser. When she finally returned to her kingdom, she was welcomed back joyfully. Everyone was eager to see the treasure the sage had given her.

During a grand ceremony, Aanya opened the box. Inside was a single, beautiful seed. The people were puzzled. 'A seed? How can this be the greatest treasure?' they murmured.

I echoed their surprise, 'A seed?'

'Yes,' my mother continued patiently, 'and listen to what happens next.'

Aanya smiled and said, 'This seed represents potential and growth. Just as a single seed can grow into a huge tree, providing shelter, food and beauty, so too can the wisdom we cultivate grow within us, shaping our lives and the world around us.'

She planted the seed in the palace garden, and over the years, it grew into a magnificent tree. Under its shade, Aanya ruled her kingdom with wisdom and compassion, always remembering the lessons she had learned from the sage. The brave princess' kingdom flourished, and her legacy of courage, wisdom and kindness lived on.

After the story, Maa asked, 'What do you understand from this story?' I tried but struggled to find an answer. She then explained, 'The moral is to emphasize the importance of learning, personal growth and leading with empathy and understanding. The knowledge the princess nurtured over time became her greatest treasure.'

There's something truly wonderful about stories, isn't there? They have this magical ability to transport us to far-off lands, ignite our imaginations and connect us with the people we love. For me, the tale of Princess Aanya is still relevant. Every time my mother related it, I found myself stepping into the shoes of that brave princess. With each twist and turn in her adventures, I felt filled with courage and an insatiable thirst for wisdom. It was more than just a story with a lesson embedded within.

For me, those storytelling sessions were such adventures. Each tale was a new journey waiting to unfold. The tale of Aanya taught me resilience, that challenges are just stepping stones on the path to greatness. These stories imbued in me an appreciation for knowledge. Wisdom is not just found in books; it's woven into the fabric of our experiences. But beyond the lessons learned, those moments formed a loving bond between my mother and me. They allowed us to share our dreams and values in a place where the troubles of the real world faded away.

At an early age, I exhibited a flair for dramatics. I loved to perform little skits and dances for the family, often enlisting Didi and the neighbour's children as my co-stars. The courtyard of our home was often transformed into a makeshift stage, with old bedsheets serving as curtains and handmade props crafted by the children. Naturally, I took the lead, directing my little troupe with authority and infectious energy. These performances, whether imitating scenes from movies or creating original stories, were the ground on which grew my passion for the arts.

Dance, Dance and Just Dance . . .

My fascination with dance began during the festivals that filled the streets of Munger with colour and music. Every year, during Durga Puja and Diwali, the town came alive with cultural performances. I watched in awe as dancers moved gracefully at these events, their costumes shimmering under the festive lights. I felt a magnetic pull towards dance and would imitate the performers. Recognizing my budding interest, my mother enrolled me in a local dance school when I was around six or seven years old.

Despite the physical and mental demands, I found joy and fulfilment in dance. It became my passion and escape. The beats of the tabla and the melodies of the sitar resonated deeply within me, guiding me through every spin and leap.

Soon, I began performing at local events and school functions. Have you ever felt that electrifying mix of nervousness and excitement before stepping onto a stage? It's a feeling like no other, one that I experienced for the first time during a cultural festival in Munger. As I stood backstage, my heart raced with anticipation. My costume, a beautiful silk sari in shades of red and gold, shimmered under the backstage lights. The jewellery and the flowers adorning me enhanced my appearance. Despite my excitement, I couldn't shake off my nerves. My palms were sweaty, and I kept adjusting my anklets to ensure they were secure. I glanced at my mother, who stood by for support. Maa's smile and gentle squeeze of the hand calmed me down. Rohit, was there too, offering words of encouragement. 'You've got this, Manisha! Remember how amazing you are,' he said, his eyes sparkling with pride. His belief in my abilities gave me an extra boost of confidence

I heard the sounds of laughter and whispers from the audience settling into their seats and feel the weight of the attention they would direct towards me. It was a moment where dreams collided with reality—a moment that marked the beginning of my journey into performance.

Stepping onto the stage as the first notes of the music filled the air, I was enveloped in a dual wave of exhilaration and apprehension. With each beat, I became a vessel for the story I was about to tell, my body flowing elegantly. The audience had their eyes fixed on my every move, and when the final note echoed, they rose to their feet and erupted into applause. That moment marked a significant turn in my journey: I came to understand just how deeply dance could create a powerful connection between the artist and those who witness the art.

As I continued to perform, my passion for dance grew with every step I took on stage. I delved into various dance styles, such as contemporary and folk, and so enriched my skill set and broadened my artistic expression. I envisioned a future where I would not only pursue a career as a professional dancer but also establish my own dance academy, a place where I could inspire and nurture the same love for dance in others that had been ignited in me.

Dance became a fundamental aspect of who I was, shaping my character in profound ways. It instilled in me a sense of discipline, highlighted the significance of expressing oneself and bolstered my self-esteem. It brought moments of joy, while in tougher times, it provided solace and companionship. My formative years were enriched by the love of a tight-knit family, the thrill of exploring new interests and the nurturing of my interests. Our home often hosted family gatherings—relatives would drop by frequently, filling the space with laughter, music and, of course, dance. Celebrations like Diwali and Holi transformed our home into a spectacle adorned with twinkling lights and fragrant flowers, while the enticing scent of home-cooked delicacies wafted through the air. My siblings and I eagerly participated in the preparations by helping set the stage for these occasions. Together, we engaged in traditional rituals, followed by sumptuous feasts and cultural performances, where my dancing took centre stage, becoming a source of pride and joy for our entire family.

At the age of seven, my imagination was a tapestry woven from fairy tales, daring escapades, the wonders of everyday life and a deep love for dance. These flights of fancy not only brought me immense entertainment but also fuelled my real-life dreams, transforming my childhood into a magical experience. Each adventure I envisioned played a crucial role in shaping my identity allowing me to explore every part of the realms of creativity in the years to come.

My parents believed in the importance of community service, and passed down this principle to us. Our family actively participated in various local initiatives, which instilled in me a sense of social responsibility. Growing up in a nurturing home and surrounded by the rich culture of Munger laid a solid foundation for my aspirations and passions. Those formative years were not just about personal discovery; they were also about the warmth of family connections and the joy of shared experiences. All of helped to shape me into the compassionate and talented person I would eventually become.

As the years passed, my enthusiasm for dance blossomed into a profound passion. I dedicated countless hours to honing my skills, learning various dance styles and striving for perfection in each. This commitment began to bear fruit, as I gained recognition not only within my local community but also in surrounding areas. Invitations to perform at cultural festivals and competitions came in more frequently; I greeted each opportunity with open arms, eager to display my artistry and share my love for dance with others.

With each performance, I discovered that dance transcended mere recreation; for me, it became a powerful medium for expressing my innermost feelings without uttering a single word. I experienced joy in every movement, from the sharp precision of my footwork to the graceful fluidity of my gestures, and this joy helped me connect with the audience. Each dance was not just a display of skill but a heartfelt communication that allowed me to forge an emotional bond with those who watched, making every moment on stage truly special.

My family members have consistently been my most steadfast supporters throughout my journey. My mother, in particular, takes immense pride in the progress I have made. Eyes filled with delight and admiration, she frequently reflects on the early days of my childhood, recalling how I would joyfully dance around our home. Watching my passion bloom, she dedicated herself to nurturing it by arranging additional dance classes and encouraging me to engage in numerous performances.

My father has also been an integral part of my growth as a dancer. Though he often expresses his support in a quiet manner, his presence has been invaluable to me. He ensured that I had all the resources necessary to pursue my passion, whether it involved driving me to dance lessons or staying up late to watch my rehearsals. His words of encouragement still resonate deeply with me: 'Manisha, pursue your passion. Dance is your true calling, and we are here to back you every step of the way.'

Rohit, my brother, stands out as my most enthusiastic supporter. As we matured, our relationship grew stronger, marked by a deep mutual respect and admiration. He often playfully refers to himself as my 'manager', assisting me in preparing for performances. The light-hearted exchanges and cherished moments we share continue to infuse our home with happiness and laughter, and reinforce the bond we have cultivated over the years.

As I entered my teenage years, I encountered the usual hurdles of simultaneously managing my education, family life and my deep love for dance. I take great pride in having achieved academic success while also putting significant time into my artistic pursuits. My dedication did not go unnoticed—both my teachers and classmates saw how I balanced various obligations, and I found myself becoming an object of admiration to many within the school community.

Now or Never!

An early landmark in my dance journey came when I was selected to perform at a prestigious national dance competition. It was a major opportunity, and I knew it would be a stepping stone toward becoming a professional dancer. The competition was intense, with participants from all over the country showcasing their talent.

I was ready and determined to give everything I had. On the day of the competition, standing behind the curtain, I was enveloped by a whirlwind of excitement and anxiety. Taking a deep breath, I remembered the countless hours I had dedicated to practice, the strong support from my family and the passion I had developed for dance. As I stepped into the spotlight, the audience hushed, and the music began to play. With each movement, I danced with both elegance and assurance; my performance intertwined technical skill with heartfelt expression.

The audience was spellbound and applauded as I concluded my routine. The judges offered their commendations, and in that moment, I experienced a profound, inexpressible sense of achievement. Although I did not secure the first place title, I gained something far more significant—a deeper understanding of my capabilities and a revitalized resolve to chase my aspirations. This experience solidified my belief in the importance of perseverance and the pleasure of pursuing what I love, no matter the outcome.

My activities extended well beyond the competition stage. I seized every chance to enhance my skills as a dancer, enrolling myself in workshops, experimenting with various dance forms and even creating my own choreography. With each experience, my dream of establishing a dance academy became more definite, and I began to map out a future where I could train and motivate aspiring dancers. Throughout this journey, I stayed true to the principles my parents taught me. I actively participated in community projects; performing at fundraising events or teaching dance to children in need gave me a deep sense of satisfaction.

My teenage years were marked by growth, both as a dancer and as a person. The lessons I learned from my family, my experiences and from dance itself all shaped me, I believe, into a sharp and compassionate young woman.

Separation of My Parents

As time passed, an unsettling darkness began to penetrate our once joyful home. The lively exchanges between my parents dwindled, giving way to a stark silence that even the cheerful laughter of their children could not dispel. The air became thick with unspoken tensions, and the echoes of unresolved disputes grew louder, overshadowing the joyous spirit of our family life. The warmth of our household slowly faded, replaced by a palpable discomfort that lingered in every corner.

Ultimately, the widening differences and persistent conflicts reached a breaking point. In a heart-wrenching turn of events, my parents made the painful choice to part ways, believing that this separation might restore some semblance of peace and stability to their existence. Their decision, though difficult, came from a desire to find clarity and healing, both for themselves and for us, their children.

The aftermath of the separation could only be tumultuous for the family. Our once harmonious household was now divided, leaving the children to confront the complexities of their new circumstances. Rohit and I made the decision to stay with our mother, relocating to her family home in Jamalpur, while our elder siblings chose to remain with Baba in Munger. As the youngest members of the family, we were still reliant on our mother's nurturing presence, and the bond between Rohit and me grew even stronger during this time. The move from Munger to Jamalpur was not without its problems, yet it also marked a fresh start.

Our mother, determined to provide a stable and loving environment despite this upheaval, worked tirelessly to ensure that we felt secure in our new home. She faced the difficulties head-on, helping us adjust to the changes. Meanwhile, our father Manoj, a man of strict principles yet deep affection, found himself in a precarious position. He now had to juggle the responsibilities of managing the household, while also tending to his own emotional issues. The separation left a deep mark on our family, especially us children, who had to grapple with feelings of confusion and sadness as we tried to make sense of our altered lives.

The emotional toll of the separation hung heavily on me—I experienced a range of feelings that included confusion, sorrow and a profound sense of incompleteness. These emotions became a constant feature of my daily life, shaping my thoughts and actions. I turned to dance, where I found a outlet for my feelings. Through movement, I was able to express the turmoil within me, channelling my feelings into something beautiful and transformative.

Dance became not just a form of expression, but a vital part of my healing process, allowing me to reclaim a sense of agency in an uncertain world.

3

Survival Amidst Separation

The early days were marked by acute sorrow. My mother found herself overwhelmed by the pain of her marriage's collapse and the distance from her elder children. The nights were the most difficult, as the stillness amplified her feelings of isolation and grief. For Rohit and me, relocating to Jamalpur was an unsettling experience. We longed for our father and elder siblings, and the unfamiliar surroundings only heightened our sense of loss and disconnection.

The initial months following the separation were a period of adjustment for both the parents and their children. Each member of the family encountered their own, unique challenges, yet they all had to come to terms with their new reality. For my brother and me, this process was particularly tough, as we deeply missed the presence of our father. The weekends became a beacon of hope for us, as they covered the time we would reunite and spend with Baba. However, these visits were a clash of emotions: while we felt joy in being together, we were also constantly reminded of where we stood now as a family.

Thus, these reunions, though filled with happiness, carried a harsh undertone. Each time we came together, the joy of reconnecting was tinged with the awareness that our time was limited, and soon we would have to part ways again. This looming sense of departure created a bittersweet atmosphere in our gatherings. However, the experience ultimately strengthened our family bond, as we learned to navigate this new chapter together, supporting one another through the emotional ups and downs that came with it.

My elder sister and brother had to mature quickly, taking on additional responsibilities at home. They helped with household chores, managed their studies and supported Baba. They missed Maa, Rohit and me deeply.

Mother, Kids and Responsibilities

Maa was deeply concerned about the emotional and psychological impact of the separation on us. She wondered how we would cope with the absence of our father and elder siblings and how we would adjust to our new life in Jamalpur. The separation of our parents cast my family into two different worlds, each grappling with its own set of challenges. For Rohit and me in Jamalpur and Sarika and Bhai in Munger, those months were marked by confusion, adaptation and, ultimately, resilience.

Baba faced tests each day as he juggled his job alongside the mounting responsibilities at home. His mornings began before dawn, as he prepared breakfast and ensured that his children were ready for school. The rush to work was a familiar but still onerous routine. After a long day at work, his evenings were consumed with helping with homework, cooking meals and tackling the various chores that piled up. Amidst all this activity, Baba leaned on his eldest son and his daughter, Sarika, to help maintain some semblance of order in their household.

Sarika often tried to lighten the mood with her cheerful calls from the kitchen, announcing, 'Papa, I have made dinner.' Her voice, filled with pride at her work, was a bittersweet reminder to Baba of the domestic responsibilities she had taken on at such a young age. Each time he responded with gratitude, he felt a pang of sorrow knowing that his daughter was shouldering a burden that should not have been hers to bear. The weight of our family's situation pressed down on him, and he wished for a way to ease her load while still managing his own. Baba tried to be emotionally available for his children, understanding they were all navigating a painful journey. He listened to our concerns, often sharing stories from his own childhood, and encouraged us to focus on our studies and hobbies.

But the dynamics of our family had shifted dramatically; it resembled a finely tuned machine that had begun to falter. The separation from Sarika and Bhai in Munger had left a noticeable void. Rohit and I found ourselves struggling to keep pace with our studies in the face of the emotional distress that surrounded us. Maa understood the importance of education and did her best to assist our learning at home. She spent time each day teaching us basic subjects and giving us basic knowledge about the environment and societal norms.

Meanwhile, our siblings in Munger were forced to step up and take on new roles that affected both their academic performance and their emotional health. The strain of these changes was palpable, and it became clear that the bonds of family, while durable, were being tested in ways that none of us had foreseen.

In Jamalpur, when school was not in session, Rohit and I found ourselves wandering through the busy neighbourhood each morning. The bustling markets and winding alleys were a treasure trove of new experiences, filling our days with things to do. The lively atmosphere there served as a welcome distraction from our homesickness. We delighted in observing the vendors as they laid out their colourful arrays of fruits and vegetables. However, our hearts would often ache when we spotted a familiar fruit, reminding us of home and the loved ones we missed dearly. During one of our visits to the market, I couldn't help but exclaim, 'Look at all those fruits, Rohit!' The sight sparked a wave of nostalgia in me. 'Do you think Papa, Bhai and Sarika are enjoying mangoes today?' I mused, my thoughts going back to family moments shared over our favourite fruit. Rohit's response was filled with a sense of longing that matched mine as he replied, 'I hope so. I miss them.' In those moments, the vibrant market around us faded slightly, overshadowed by the warmth of our memories and the ache of separation.

As the sun set and the day faded into night, Maa would gather us for storytelling sessions that transported us to far-off lands filled with brave warriors, noble princesses and wondrous mythical creatures. These tales were not merely an evening diversion; they were a source of comfort and inspiration, lifting our spirits and nurturing our resilience. 'Tell us more about the brave princess again, Maa,' I would eagerly request, my eyes sparkling with anticipation. My mother's storytelling created a safe haven for us, helping to ease our turbulent emotions and fostering hope in our hearts.

Gradually, we began to settle down a bit. Making new friends helped a lot. Rohit and I learnt new games local to the area and this made us feel more a part of the new community. The routines we established, the friends we made and the hobbies we developed helped us navigate that difficult period in Jamalpur. In Munger, my siblings found comfort in one another as they fought their shared grief. Their connection was strengthened by their reminiscences about our mother, Rohit and me, as they created understanding among themselves despite their sorrow. Each evening, they would engage in heartfelt conversations, recounting cherished memories that kept the essence of our family alive.

My sister often reflected on how much they missed the vibrant energy that we younger children brought into our home. It was not uncommon for Baba to find Sarika in my room, tenderly clutching my beloved doll, a memento of the happiness that once filled their lives. One evening, as the weight of silence enveloped the house, my elder brother, Rahul Raj, voiced what they all felt. 'I miss their noise, Baba,' he confessed, his voice heavy with longing. Baba, ever the pillar of strength, placed a comforting hand on his son's shoulder and replied, 'I do too, but we must remain strong for one another.' He made it a priority to be emotionally present for his children on the difficult path they were all traversing. By sharing stories from his own past and encouraging them to work on their studies and enjoy their hobbies, Baba aimed to remind them that even in their darkest moments, they were not alone.

Maa became our pillar of strength. She encouraged Rohit and me to have open conversations and to express our feelings to each other. Her constant reassurance and endless love provided us with the emotional support we needed to navigate that dark period. Didi and Dada became closer to Baba. They found strength in each other, sharing their hopes and fears. This bond helped them endure the difficult period of adjustment.

'We'll get through this, won't we, Baba?' his elder son asked one night, looking up.

'Yes, we will,' Manoj replied, his voice firm. 'As long as we stick together.'

After enduring months apart from them, Manoj felt an overwhelming urge to reconnect with his younger children. With a heart bearing both hope and anxiety, he proceeded towards Jamalpur. He was acutely aware that the time spent in separation had inflicted deep emotional wounds, and he braced himself for the possibility of resistance from those he loved. The thought of facing their pain troubled him, but the desire to reunite and heal those wounds bore him onward.

Upon arriving, Manoj took time to articulate his feelings and the motivations behind the decision he had taken: to bring us back to Munger. Ragini, despite her own heartache, acknowledged the depth of our father's love for us. She understood that this choice, though difficult, might restore some stability to our lives. With tears in her eyes, Ragini implored, 'Promise me you'll take good care of them, Manoj. They are my world.' To which Manoj solemnly replied, 'I promise, Ragini.' We gathered our belongings and headed back to Munger, riven with conflicting emotions: hope, sadness and the anticipation of better things.

The route from Jamalpur to Munger was a mere eight kilometres and usually took twenty to twenty-five minutes. However, that day, time seemed to crawl. Both of us were teary-eyed, distressed as we were by the separation from our mother. As soon as we reached Munger and stepped into our home, the sound of our footsteps and the jingling of my anklet alerted Sarika and our elder brother Rahul. They rushed to the door, and we four siblings hugged each other tightly, bursting into tears.

Sarika and Bhai, being a bit older, were acutely aware of the seriousness of the situation—their parents had separated and it had been quite some time since they had seen either of us. The emotional reunion after such a long absence overwhelmed them, and they embraced Rohit and me tightly, tears streaming down their faces. In contrast, Rohit and I, being younger, did not fully comprehend the weight of our move back. But still, while we felt a sense of joy at being reunited with our father and siblings, our hearts were heavy with sorrow for Maa, and we wondered how we would live without her presence.

Observing the children in distress, Baba, frustrated, snapped at Didi, 'What's happening here? Enough with the tears! Get everyone inside and ask your aunt to prepare some tea. Stop this nonsense.' I saw that Didi was taken aback by his harsh tone, but she quickly composed herself and ushered all of us indoors. Baba's request was rejected by our aunt with the curt reply, 'I'm busy right now. Why don't you make the tea yourself?'

Although Sarika had a tuition class scheduled soon, she chose to forgo it that day to be with her siblings. Taking the chore upon herself, she brewed tea for everyone, including our father, aunt, uncle and grandparents. Once the tea was served, she settled down with us, eager to learn more about our mother's welfare. Rohit and I were too young to convey our mother's feelings accurately or explain the situation. Like innocent children, we simply said, 'Maa is fine. Maa is very good.' We didn't understand why our parents were no longer together, and as we were closer to our mother, we kept asking, 'When will Maa come?'

For Sarika and Bhai, the beginning was incredibly tough. They had come to terms with the fact that their mother might never return home, but explaining this to their younger siblings without saddening them was quite beyond their capabilities. Since Sarika and our elder brother didn't go to tuition that day, we four siblings started playing together. Hearing my voice, some neighbourhood children joined them, and we all began playing tag.

Time would move forward; I would grow older and more responsible, but I never stopped missing my mother and longing to see her again.

I went back to school. My classmates bombarded me with questions, asking where I had been and why I hadn't come to school earlier. I replied, 'I went to my grandmother's house. I didn't have to go to school there. My dad brought me back yesterday, so I had to come to school today. It was so much fun there; I played all day, had a little tuition and then had the rest of the day off.' The first period started, and everyone began studying.

I was naturally playful and mischievous and often got into small squabbles with my peers over trivial prizes like books or chalk. But I didn't hold grudges and would forget any arguments by the next day, happily playing with everyone again. Soon I was helping Sarika with household chores. Although we did well in our studies, we siblings diligently helped with household tasks, assisted Baba and cared for our grandparents. As the youngest son, Rohit didn't have many responsibilities and spent most of his time enjoying himself. But as time went on, Didi, Bhai and I took on increasingly more domestic responsibilities.

Growing up didn't mean giving up on listening to stories. Dadi, our grandmother had stepped into our mother's shoes and become the family storyteller. One night, after dinner, Rohit and I were squabbling as siblings often do when Dadi called from her room saying, 'Why are both of you fighting? Don't you want to hear a story tonight? I have a very interesting one.' That was enough for both of us to forget the fight. Rohit raced to her room while I went to the kitchen to fetch Dadi a drink of water as I always did before a story. I had picked up this habit from the time Maa used to tell us stories. She would always get thirsty in the middle, so to avoid interruptions, I would prepare a jug of water beforehand.

When I carried the pitcher into Dadi's room, she smiled and said, 'Manisha, you never forget to bring water.' I laughed and said, 'Grandma, start the story. You might get thirsty, and then you'd stop the story.

It's better to have water ready so the story can continue uninterrupted.'

Dadi laughed heartily and sat on the bed. Rohit and I positioned ourselves on the carpet near the bed, eagerly waiting for the story. I loved stories so much that I didn't mind hearing the same one twice, but Rohit always wanted a new story. If Dadi started a story he had already heard, he would insist on hearing a new one.

Just like every other time, our grandmother began, 'Once upon a time, there was a wolf living near the forests of Telipura. This wolf was very dominant and would scare and bully all the other animals in the forest.' As she continued, Rohit interrupted, 'Stop, Grandma! You've told us this one before. Tell us a new story. This one is old.'

Amused, Dadi teased him, 'All right, all right, sit down. I won't repeat the same story. Stay here, don't go away.'

After a moment, she began, 'In a quaint village, there once lived a king who was the proud father of four sons and a daughter. The royal children were affectionately referred to as the princes and the princess, and each carried the weight of their father's high expectations. The king dedicated himself to training his sons in the art of warfare, imparting knowledge about various weapons and combat techniques. Every year, the village hosted an archery competition, a contest the king had dominated for years. However, this time, he harboured a different wish—he felt no desire to win the accolade for himself and instead longed for one of his sons to claim victory.'

Curiosity sparked within me as I turned to my grandmother and asked, 'What exactly is archery?' With a warm smile, she explained, 'Archery is a sport that involves using a bow to shoot arrows at targets. Think of Lord Rama, who wielded a bow with great skill to strike his targets. That's the essence of archery.' I nodded in understanding and encouraged her to continue with the tale.

'As the king rigorously trained his sons for the upcoming competition, an unseen observer lurked in the shadows, a spy who watched their every move from behind a jamun tree. Initially unaware of the spy's presence, the king's attention was drawn when his sons reported seeing the figure lurking nearby. They expressed their concerns: "Father, we often notice someone hiding behind the tree, watching us intently. He always departs before we do. While he hasn't harmed us, we fear he may be a spy for our rivals." The king pondered their words, acknowledging the possibility of a plot against them. He reassured his sons, stating, "While it's true someone may be watching, remember that our skills and knowledge are ours alone; they cannot be taken away." With renewed determination, the princes returned to their training, mindful of their father's wisdom. As the day of the competition dawned, participants from nearby villages arrived, eager to compete for the coveted golden bow and arrow, a symbol of prowess in marksmanship. Despite the king's hopes and encouragement, his sons had not taken their archery practice as seriously as he had wished.

'As the sun rose high in the sky, the arena buzzed with excitement and spectators filled the stands. The king's soldiers and attendants scurried about, ensuring that everything was in place for the grand event. Just as the competition was about to commence, the king's sons spotted a familiar figure among the participants—a man who bore a striking resemblance to the suspected spy. They turned to their father, exclaiming, "Father, look! That man is the same one who used to observe us!" The king, however, remained composed and replied, "We cannot jump to conclusions. Whoever he is, he has never caused us harm. Many will be watching you today; we cannot label them all as spies." The king's sons, still uneasy pointed out that the man had now entered the competition. The king, maintaining his calm demeanour, reassured them, "It is of no consequence. Every individual has the right to compete. If he possesses the skill of a good archer, then he should certainly be allowed to participate." With that, the atmosphere shifted as the competition kicked off, and each archer was given the opportunity to demonstrate their talent.

'The archers took their turns, showcasing their abilities with varying degrees of success. The second round introduced a challenging task: each competitor had to shoot an arrow at a spinning coconut suspended in the air, aiming to split it cleanly in two. Many faltered, unable to hit the target, but the tension in the air grew as the king's sons took their turns. One by one, they stepped up, demonstrating their training and skill. However, only two of the four sons managed to strike the coconut, and none succeeded in splitting it apart. The crowd watched these failed shots with disappointment.

'The spectators realized that none of the archers had successfully split the coconut yet, and only one competitor was left. Since the king had not participated this time, everyone felt that no archer could match the king's skills. Meanwhile, the last competitor stepped forward with his bow and arrow, preparing to take aim. By this time, the spectators had lost interest, as all the renowned archers had failed. They had little hope for this unknown competitor. However, to everyone's astonishment, the final competitor not only hit the coconut but also split it cleanly into two halves with his arrow. The audience applauded and cheered, appreciating the new archer's remarkable skill.

'The king's sons felt envious of this man. The king then called the competitor to the stage to honour him and presented him with the golden bow and arrow. The competitor expressed his gratitude and began to leave the stage. As he was descending, the king called out, "Wait! You haven't told us your name. We've never seen you before. Who are you, and where do you come from? If the winner leaves without revealing his identity, what message will that send to the people?"

'Upon hearing this, the archer removed his mask, revealing his identity to the spectators, the competitors and the king. To everyone's surprise, the archer was none other than the princess, the king's own daughter. The entire audience was stunned. The king asked his daughter, "When did you learn to shoot so well? I've never seen you practise, so how did you manage this?"

'The princess replied, "Father, I've been watching you practise archery since I was a child. Every year, seeing you win this competition filled me with joy. I always wished I could become a great archer like you."

'The king responded, "That's okay, but how did you learn to shoot an arrow so well without practising?" The king's daughter replied, "Every day when you taught my four brothers archery, I would watch from a distance. I would then practise at night in the garden behind the palace while everyone was asleep. I was afraid someone might see me; no girl in our village had ever taken up archery. But I loved it, so I continued in secret. Today, I thought I would enter the competition disguised as a boy. It is thanks to your teaching that I could do this." Hearing this, the king's eyes filled with tears. He said, "I worked so hard to teach my four sons archery, but despite all that effort, they could not master it. Yet, you learnt it just by watching from a distance. I announce that from now on, not only men but also women and girls from our village can participate in this competition. Furthermore, my daughter will teach archery to any woman who wants to learn." That night, there was a grand celebration in the palace, and happiness spread everywhere.'

'So, what did you learn from this story, Manisha?' Dadi asked. I replied, 'Dadi, I learnt that we should learn archery from a distance to avoid getting hurt.' Dadi laughed and said, 'No, dear, that's not it. The princess watched from a distance because people believed that girls could not practise archery. She feared that if she tried to learn openly, people would mock her or prevent her from learning. But she had a strong desire to learn, so she mastered archery by watching from afar and refining her craft in secret. Remember, she didn't just watch; she worked on her skill diligently every night. That's how she succeeded.'

Then Dadi asked Rohit, 'What did you learn, Rohit?' But there was no response. I shook Rohit and asked, 'Rohit, are you asleep?' Indeed, Rohit had fallen asleep. We both laughed loudly. Dadi then said, 'Come on, Manisha, it's time for you to sleep too. We'll continue with another story tomorrow.'

Thinking about the stories I had heard, I discovered a profound, unforeseen transformation within myself. Each tale resonated deeply in my mind and heart. The narrative shared above is crafted for my younger audience and those who dare to dream. Just as the princess toiled her way to success, we too must dedicate ourselves to the pursuit of our ambitions. This story left a mark on me—it ignited a spark of inspiration that I hadn't realized was there.

Little did I know, my journey was paralleling that of the princess, with its own set of trials and victories waiting to be revealed in the coming chapters of my life. The challenges that I have faced are not unlike those faced by the characters in the tales I cherish. Each experience, whether trying or exhilarating, contributes to my growth and understanding and shapes the person I am destined to become. The lessons served by these narratives are guiding lights, encouraging me to strive for greatness.

4

A Daughter's Choice

The household stirred to life under the commanding call of my grandmother, Dadi—a figure of tradition and strength who leaned on her granddaughters for help. 'Manisha and Sarika, rise and shine!' her voice rang out, cutting through the stillness of the early morning. 'We have a busy day ahead before you head off to school.'

'Yes, Dadi,' we both replied, stifling our yawns as we rolled out of our shared bed. With a practised routine, we splashed water on our faces, braided our hair neatly and made our way to the kitchen. There, alongside our grandmother, we engaged in the familiar morning ritual of cooking breakfast and preparing lunch for the family. The aroma of sizzling food mingled with the sound of clattering dishes, creating a symphony of morning activity. 'Manisha, did you remember to pack your lunch?' Sarika asked, as she moved on to diligently scrubbing the kitchen floor. 'Yes, and I've made yours too,' I responded cheerfully, placing our lunchboxes on the counter.

Dadi was the matriarch of our family, both affectionate and authoritative; her adherence to traditional values shaped our daily lives. Her love for us was deep, yet it came with a strictness that left no room for deviation from the customs she held dear. In our home, how daughters should conduct and present themselves was firmly established. Dadi believed that the way we dressed reflected our family's honour and integrity, and she enforced a strict dress code based on modesty. I can still hear her voice, reminding me that sleeveless tops were out of the question and that my dupatta must always be draped just so. 'Make sure it's arranged properly,' she would insist, her eyes narrowing as I prepared to step outside. I would nod obediently, adjusting my dupatta to align with her high standards, feeling the weight of tradition resting on my shoulders.

Yet, beneath the layers of tradition, my heart beat for fashion; this passion thrived secretly in the shadows of Dadi's watchful gaze. On those rare evenings when Baba and the rest of the family were out late, I found a temporary freedom that allowed me to indulge in my secret love for style. With a mix of excitement and guilt, I would pull out a dress I had stashed away, hidden from Dadi's eyes, slip it on and feel a rush of exhilaration as I admired my reflection. 'Just for a little while,' I would whisper to myself, savouring the moment before the inevitable return of my family. As this return approached, I would fold my beloved dress with care and tuck it away, and hurriedly change back into my regular attire, longing for the day when I could express my true self without fear of disapproval.

Now in the tenth grade, I had mastered the art of multitasking. My days were a rush of activity; each began before dawn and extended late into the night. I fetched water from the nearby well, assisted Sarika with meal preparation and ensured the house was perfectly clean before leaving for school. Our elder brother, a college student still living at home, managed the grocery shopping and outdoor chores, while I attended to cleaning and laundry. Despite having such a demanding home life, I dedicated myself to my academic pursuits, often sacrificing sleep to study late into the night, writing assignments and preparing for exams.

As my responsibilities at home multiplied, finding time to attend dance classes became quite a task. Dadi held firmly to her traditional views—she considered dance a mere distraction from my obligations and studies. She would sternly urge me to prioritize my studies and household tasks above all else. Baba too shared this view. Nevertheless, the weekends offered a brief escape, allowing me to dance. I would lose myself in the beat of my favourite routines, watching videos of renowned dancers and eagerly studying their techniques to enhance my own skills. My room was adorned with colourful posters of my dance idols, each one a symbol of my aspirations. In those moments on the weekends, I felt a sense of joy and freedom, and refreshed my passion for dance, despite the weight of my responsibilities.

My journey into the world of Kathak began when I was just seven or eight years old. I was fascinated by the graceful movements of the dancers, and the rhythm of the tabla that seemed to echo in my very soul. The allure of this beautiful dance form led me to approach my father with a hopeful request: 'Baba, can I learn Kathak?' Sensing my passion, Baba responded with a gentle smile, promising, 'If you do well in school and help out at home, we can make it happen.'

Despite the financial hurdles we faced, he remained committed to supporting my dreams—he had me enrolled in Kathak classes, fully aware of the joy that lit up my face whenever I spoke of dance. However, as I delved deeper into the dance form, I began to sense my grandmother's growing disapproval of my pursuits. Her stern gaze often troubled my heart, yet I found comfort in memories of my mother, who had once spun tales that inspired my love for movement and expression. One story that particularly resonated with me was about a little girl named Meera, who lived in a village strikingly similar to my own. Through her journey, I rediscovered the beauty and freedom that dance could bring.

Meera was fascinated by the dance of fireflies, their tiny lights flickering like earthbound stars. An old woman had told her, 'The fireflies are drawn to joy and lightness of heart. If you let your heart guide you, you will dance as they do, with freedom and grace.' Inspired by this story, Meera began to dance in the fields, her movements mirroring the graceful arcs of the fireflies. Soon, she became known throughout the village as the girl who danced with the fireflies.

This story appealed to me, for I saw striking similarities between my life and that of Meera. Despite the relentless demands of my daily routine, I remained committed to Kathak, a passion I now had to pursue in secrecy. Aware that Dadi would not approve, I cleverly crafted excuses to slip away from home. I would leave under the guise of running errands, only to change into my dance attire the moment I arrived at the studio.

In a home where tradition reigned supreme, Sarika Didi and I discovered a brief yet exhilarating taste of freedom during our secretive trips to see Maa in Jamalpur. These moments served as a reprieve from the rigid standards of our upbringing, allowing us to reconnect with our mother. Each month, Didi and I would carefully orchestrate our visits, ensuring we remained unnoticed because Dadi did not approve. We spun elaborate tales for Dadi, pretending we were off to a friend's house for a study session; we would even skip classes entirely to steal precious hours with Maa in the quiet of the early morning.

The ride to Jamalpur was a blend of thrill and trepidation, but the thought of being with our mother made every bump in the road worthwhile. 'Hold on tight,

Manisha,' Didi would remind me as our autorickshaw jolted along the uneven path. 'I always do,' I would reply, my fingers gripping the edge of the seat. Once we arrived, we would engage in heartfelt conversations, sharing news from Munger and our small daily victories. My mother listened with full attention, offering wise advice. 'Stay strong and believe in yourself,' she would encourage us after absorbing our stories. 'Always remember that you are stronger than you think.'

But soon, it would be time to return. We would sneak back home as quietly as we had left, hoping Dadi and Baba would not notice our absence from school. Back at home, we resumed our roles in the household as if nothing had happened, but the warmth of our mother's embrace and her encouraging words stayed with us, giving us much strength. These secretive outings were not just about the joy of reunion—they were lifelines that provided us sisters with a sense of belonging and emotional support in a world that often felt constricting. The thrill of our covert adventures, coupled with our mother's affection, etched each visit in our hearts. These visits to Jamalpur affirmed our unbreakable bond with Maa. Through them, we found the strength to navigate our strict household atmosphere, pursue our passions and hold onto our dreams.

As my final exams drew near, my daily routine intensified significantly. It was exhausting, balancing household chores, academic responsibilities and my secret dance classes. I found myself studying late into the night, driven by a fierce determination to achieve top marks. In these quiet hours, while the rest of the world was asleep, I would pore over my books under the soft glow of a lamp, my eyelids heavy with weariness. When the exam day finally arrived, I felt both nerves and resolve. I had dedicated countless hours to prepare for this very day, and as I stepped into the examination hall, I recalled my aspirations and the unwavering support of my family. 'Just as Meera danced with the fireflies, I too will glide through these exams,' I reminded myself, drawing inspiration from my mother's tales.

The beginning of twelfth grade marked a pivotal moment for me. The pressure of upcoming board exams, combined with my household duties and Kathak practice, made that year the most challenging yet. The expectations were high, and the stakes even higher. I knew that my performance this year would shape my future.

The relentless cycle of household duties exhausted me. Dadi's deteriorating health meant I had to shoulder even more responsibilities. Each morning, Baba would inquire, 'Manisha, did you remember to give Dadi her medicine?' to which I would respond, 'Yes, Baba,' while my mind raced ahead, mapping out the day's endless tasks. Amidst these demands, I remained committed to my studies, knowing that achieving good results would help me chase my dream of becoming a dancer. I carried my textbooks with me everywhere, seizing every spare minute to immerse myself in learning. As the pressure of the impending board exams intensified, I found myself yearning for my mother's embrace and words of encouragement. I began to plan another visit to Jamalpur, hoping to derive solace and strength from her.

It was a bright Saturday morning when Didi and I embarked on our little adventure. We had cleverly informed Dadi that we were heading to school for some extra study sessions. 'We need to return by early evening,' Didi reminded me as we hopped into the autorickshaw, her voice tinged with excitement. 'I'm aware,' I replied, feeling equally excited. Upon our arrival, Maa greeted us with warmth, enveloping us in loving hugs and cuddles. As we savoured a delightful meal together, Didi and I filled Maa in on our lives back in Munger. I wasted no time diving into the pressures of being in twelfth grade, the weight of expectations bearing down on me and my secret yearning for dance. Maa listened intently, her eyes showing both pride and worry.

'*Maa, bahut zyada ho jaata hai*—sometimes, it all feels like too much,' I confessed, my voice quavering as I fought back the tears that threatened to spill. 'There's just so much to juggle, and with exams looming ahead, it feels overwhelming.' My mother took my hand, her presence a steady anchor in the storm of my emotions. 'You've always shown such determination and dedication,' she reassured me gently. 'These obstacles are merely stepping stones that will fortify your resolve.'

'But what if I can't manage everything?' I asked, searching for the comfort I desperately needed. 'You can, and you will,' my mother asserted with confidence. 'Keep your eyes on your dreams; they are your guiding light, and nothing should deter you from chasing them. Let your passion for dance be your driving force; it's what sets you apart.' Her words washed over me like a soothing balm; I realized that my love for dance was not merely an escape but a vital source of strength to help me face the challenges of my final year in school. That day became a cherished moment for us. My mother recounted her own battles, emphasizing the significance of resilience and self-belief. 'Whenever I encountered hardships, I reminded myself of my purpose,' she shared, locking eyes with me. 'Cling to your aspirations, Manisha; they will see you through even the darkest times.'

As the afternoon waned, it became time for us to return home. We hugged our mother tightly, reluctant to leave her. 'Promise me you'll take care of yourself and keep working hard,' Maa said, her eyes moist. 'I promise, Maa,' I replied in a steady voice. With heavy hearts, Didi and I boarded the autorickshaw back to Munger. The journey home was filled with quiet resolve. I replayed my mother's words in my mind, drawing strength from the love and encouragement I had received from her.

Back in Munger, I immersed myself in my studies with a renewed purpose. My mother's encouraging words resonated within me during those late-night study marathons and the following early morning routines. With a new-found focus, I harnessed my love for dance as a wellspring of motivation. My time spent in dance class took on a deeper significance—every motion and rhythm served as a poignant reminder of the commitment I had made to both my mother and myself. The mantra 'Hold onto your dreams' became my guiding principle. I learnt to quiet my thoughts, soothe my anxieties and approach the impending board exams with a serene yet resolute spirit.

The encounter with my mother just prior to the exams marked a pivotal point in my life. In that moment, I became certain that dance was my destined path, and I eagerly anticipated what lay ahead with a sense of optimism. I sat for the exams, and I performed admirably. Yet, as the months unfolded, a sensation of confinement in Munger lingered, unsettling me.

> Khudko kar buland itna ke har taqdeer se pehle khuda
> tujhse puche bata teri raza kya hai.

> (Elevate your self to such a height that before every
> destiny is written, God himself asks you, 'Tell me,
> what is your desire?')

The narrow prospects in Munger made it increasingly clear to me that remaining there would hinder me from fulfilling my aspirations. Each day was a stark reminder of these obstacles, with Dadi's stringent rules and the family's weighty expectations casting a long shadow over my ambitions. Conversations about my future revolved around either staying home or following conventional career paths, and so conforming to suffocating societal standards. As time went by, I yearned more and more to escape these constraints and began to reflect deeply on my future. I often pondered how I could chase my dreams in Munger, yet the thought of being stifled by my environment was disheartening. I longed to break free from my family's expectations and pursue a different path, but I was acutely aware that the opportunities available in Munger were very limited to those in larger cities.

The idea of leaving Munger for a more promising location grew firmer in my head. However, persuading my grandmother and father to support such a decision seemed impossible. One morning, as I busied myself with the usual household tasks, nostalgia overcame me, and I remembered my childhood friend, Priyanka, who had always dreamed of becoming a dancer. It had been a few years since she left Munger, and an intense desire to reconnect with her surged within me. I decided to reach out to her, and to my astonishment, I discovered that she was now in Kolkata, pursuing her studies alongside her passion for dance. Our conversation flowed effortlessly; she recounted the trials and triumphs of her journey, and her experiences at a dance academy and within the vibrant artistic community of Kolkata.

Listening to her, I felt a flicker of inspiration ignite within me.

Priyanka's bravery in venturing beyond her comfort zone struck a chord with me and prompted me to share my own aspirations. Her words were highly encouraging: 'You should come to Kolkata, Manisha! There's a whole world out there waiting to be explored. I was terrified at first, but stepping out of my comfort zone was the best decision I ever made. You have so much talent; you could make a name for yourself here.' Her encouragement filled me with a sense of possibility and hope. In that moment, I realized that perhaps the hurdles I faced were not as daunting as they seemed, and that taking a leap of faith could lead to a life filled with purpose and fulfilment. By the end of the call, I began to believe that I, too, could take a bold step towards my dreams. Priyanka's story and encouragement made me confident that perhaps it was time to leave Munger and seek new opportunities elsewhere. The idea of reuniting with Priyanka in Kolkata and the possibility of being roommates filled me with hope and excitement.

That night, as I lay in bed staring at the ceiling, Priyanka's words echoed in my mind. A single thought kept repeating itself: 'Why not Kolkata? If Priyanka can do it, why can't I?'

With newfound determination, I began to research dance schools and part-time job prospects in Kolkata. Seeking guidance, I turned to my dance instructor at school, and our conversation proved to be both enlightening and uplifting. My teacher shared valuable insights about prestigious dance academies in Kolkata, and generously affirmed my potential: 'Manisha, your talent is remarkable. You deserve a larger stage, and a vibrant city like Kolkata can provide the opportunities necessary for you to truly thrive.'

This conversation heightened my desire to leave Munger for the bustling city. I began to reflect on the limitations of my current life—traditional expectations surrounding attire, restrictions on my movements, the secretive trips to my mother's house and the hidden dance classes. It became clear to me that to chase my dreams and embrace my freedom, I would have to take a courageous leap. The idea of leaving home was both exhilarating and terrifying. I knew that convincing my family, especially Dadi, would be an uphill battle. I spent days rehearsing my arguments, preparing myself for the inevitable confrontation.

To my dear readers, I would like to share these moments of trepidation and exhilaration. Believe in yourself and find support from well-wishers; those who love you will always guide on the right path. Never be too cautious; don't be afraid to set off on the path of your dreams. The lessons learnt through hard work and perseverance are never lost.

5
Determined to Achieve

Schooldays

My nani's side of the family

At Bua's house

My cousin Misty's birthday celebration

On another of Misty's birthdays

Me and Sarika Di

With my brother Rahul Raj

On a trip to Darjeeling

My first dance competition in Munger

Dance competition at Bihar School of Music and Arts

Sarika Di's birthday

Celebrating Durga Pooja

Holi celebrations back home in Munger

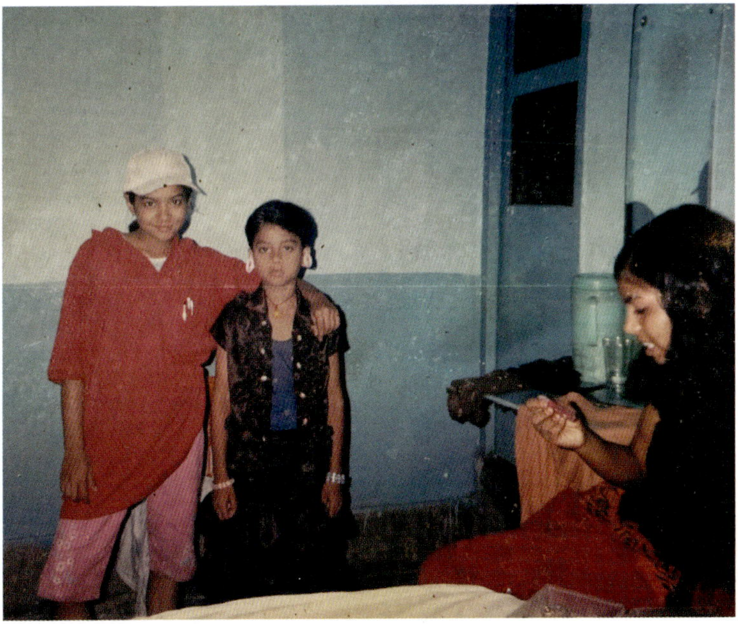

Kolkata days

Out and about on a visit to Kolkata

A dance performance on Teacher's Day

Before heading for the Durga Pooja visarjan ceremony; I was in the 7th standard

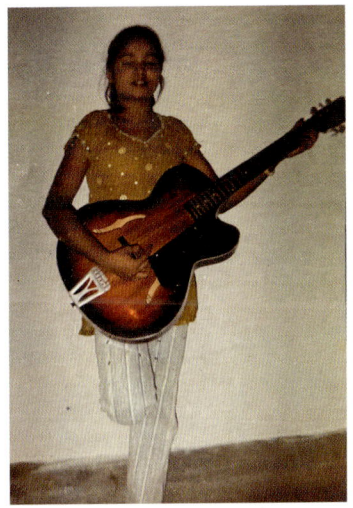

Trying something a little different from dance

Moments from Manisha's birthday celebration

Dressed up for Saraswati Pooja

Dance practice

Impromptu photoshoot

I love my *golu-molu* students to whom I used to give dance lessons

With Baba

Photoshoot post *Bigg Boss*

As a contestant on the dance show
Jhalak Dikhhla Jaa

One of my best performances

Lifting the *Jhalak Dikhhla Jaa* trophy

On the stage after our win

The first major event I attended

At *Jhalak Dikhhla Jaa*

A clip from the unreleased show *Ab Hasega India*—a project that never made it out

It was truly amazing to meet Johnny Lever

With my handsome brother and gorgeous sister

Another lovely picture with Baba

I came, I saw, I conquered their hearts!

My father had always wanted me to secure a government job; he believed that benefits like a good salary, job security and respect made it the safest and most stable path with. However, I felt a deep, unspoken desire to explore something different, something that made my heart race with excitement, although I wasn't sure what that was yet. One evening, while I sat in the small living room, lost in my thoughts, my sister Sarika noticed my distant expression. 'Are you thinking about getting a new chair?' she teased.

I smiled faintly and confessed that I did not want to pursue a government job, despite everyone's expectations; I had been feeling lost under their weight. Sarika listened intently, nodding. Our family valued stability and tradition, making my dream of becoming a dancer a daunting prospect to pursue.

'I understand, Manisha,' Sarika said softly. 'It's hard to go against what everyone expects. But you have to follow your heart. Have you thought about what you really want to do?'

I looked up, my eyes glistening with unshed tears. 'I . . . I want to dance,' I whispered, almost afraid to say it out loud. 'I want to go to Kolkata and learn from the best. But I know it's a crazy idea. We can't afford it, and Baba would never agree.' As I said this, I felt a rush of emotions—fear, excitement and a deep yearning for something more.

Sarika listened to me, her face thoughtful. Didi knew our father well enough to understand that he would likely be against such a plan. Despite this, Didi supported my expressed desire. She understood the difficulties I would face and advised me to have a plan in place before confronting our father. I felt more confident with my sister's support and decided to talk to my mother first.

As the hours of the night dragged on, sleep eluded me; a whirlwind of emotions overcame me as I contemplated the pursuit of my passion. Thoughts of potential failure and the fear of letting my family down loomed large, yet an undeniable urge to take the leap persisted within me. I decided to speak with my mother the following day, hoping she would lend her support in persuading my father to allow me to chase my dreams. The next morning, my sister and I completed our household tasks and approached our father, seeking his permission to attend a friend's birthday celebration, all while secretly planning to visit our mother. 'Make sure to come back soon,' he instructed as he headed off to work. Relieved, we set off for Jamalpur; our spirits were lifted by the anticipation of a delightful breakfast awaiting us.

After finishing our meal, I approached my mother, feeling a mix of excitement and anxiety about what I was about to share. 'Maa, do you have a moment to talk?' I asked, my voice betraying a hint of nervousness. My mother looked up from her task; her expression shifted to one of curiosity as she sensed the seriousness in my tone. She paused her dish-washing and invited me to sit down. 'Absolutely, *beta*. What's troubling you?' she inquired, her voice soothing and filled with concern. I took a moment to gather my thoughts and inhaled deeply to steady my nerves before I began to speak.

It was an important moment for me, and I wanted to convey my thoughts clearly. 'Maa, I've been reflecting on my future, and I've come to a significant realization. I don't want to pursue a government job. Instead, I have this burning desire to go to Kolkata and learn dance there. It's a passion that I can't ignore, and I feel compelled to explore it,' I explained, my voice gaining strength even as my heart raced. My mother listened carefully, her expression shifting to one of understanding as she clearly felt the fire of my aspiration. She spoke thoughtfully about the challenges that lay ahead, emphasizing the importance of being prepared for potential obstacles. Yet, her tone was not one of discouragement; rather, it was a gentle reminder of the realities I might face. I nodded. and 'I understand, Maa. But I can't shake the feeling that I need to pursue this path. I don't want to live with regrets or the haunting question of "what if". I just need the opportunity to show what I can do,' I implored, my eyes reflecting a fierce determination to chase my dreams.

My mother sighed and reached out to hold my hand. 'You're a brave girl, and I'm proud of you for wanting to follow your dreams. But you must be prepared: your father will be very upset, and you'll need to be strong,' she advised, her voice full of concern and love. 'Thank you, Maa. I'll talk to Baba, but I wanted to know if I have your support,' I said, my voice soft but hopeful. My mother nodded, with a small smile on her lips. 'You have my support, beta. I'll talk to your father and try to help him understand. But you must be prepared for his reaction.'

A wave of gratitude and relief flooded me as I realized how much my mother's cautious support meant. Her presence made the daunting challenge of seeking my father's approval feel a bit more manageable. I wrapped my arms around her, savouring the comfort of our embrace. My sister and I returned home buoyed by a sense of positivity—while the issue remained unresolved, we had the support we needed.

The rest of the day blurred into a mix of anticipation and anxiety. I struggled to focus, my mind repeatedly drifting back to the conversation I needed to have with my father. To fight this, I busied myself with various tasks, but as evening approached, the reality of the impending discussion loomed larger. I knew my father would be home soon, and I had to gather every ounce of courage to face him.

Finally, after dinner, I approached my father.

'Baba,' I began, my voice trembling slightly, 'I want to talk to you about something important.'

My father looked up from his newspaper. 'What is it, beta?'

I inhaled deeply and began to deliver the speech I had meticulously crafted. I shared my love for dance, articulated my aspirations of turning this passion into a professional career and highlighted the exciting prospects that awaited me in Kolkata. The words flowed from me, each one infused with the hope that had fuelled my dreams for so long.

As I spoke, an unsettling silence enveloped the room, thick with tension. My father's face shifted; confusion and disapproval flickered across his features. He looked at me as if he couldn't quite grasp what he had just heard. 'Dance?' he echoed, his tone serious. 'You want to squander your time and our resources on something as frivolous as dancing?' The weight of his words hung heavily in the air, and I felt my anxiety return.

Despite the turmoil inside me, I stood firm, meeting my father's intense gaze with unwavering resolve. 'Baba, this isn't a waste. It's my passion, and I genuinely believe I can forge a career from it,' I responded, striving to maintain a respectful demeanour. My father's expression hardened further as he shook his head. His voice held frustration: 'Manisha, dancing is merely a pastime, not a viable career path. We've sacrificed so much to provide you with a solid education, and now you want to throw it all away for a dream?' Tears threatened to spill from my eyes, but I fought to suppress them. 'Baba, I understand your concerns, but this means everything to me. I can't imagine living a life without joy. I need to at least give it a chance,' I pleaded, my voice quivering with emotion.

My father rose suddenly from his seat in anger. 'That's enough, Manisha! This conversation ends here. You will not be going to Kolkata. Your focus will be on preparing for a government job, and that's final,' he declared, his voice reverberating through the small dining area.

I remained motionless, tears running down my face as emotions engulfed me—rage, sorrow and an overwhelming sense of frustration. Deep down, I understood that my father cared for me and believed he was acting in my best interest, yet I struggled to comprehend his opposition to my dreams.

The next few days were filled with tension. My father barely uttered a word to me, and his disapproval loomed over our household like a dark shadow. To cope, I immersed myself in dance, spending hours perfecting my routines in the small courtyard of our home. I was determined not to let go of my aspirations, even if it meant defying my father. My mother, on the other hand, stood by me quietly; she even helped me explore dance schools in Kolkata.

One evening, while I was practising, I heard a knock at the door. Opening it, I found my uncle, my father's younger brother, standing there with a warm smile. 'I've heard about your plans, Manisha,' he said softly as he stepped inside. 'Your father told me everything.'

I felt nervous. I admired my uncle, who was smart and open-minded, but I wasn't sure if he would support me. 'Uncle, I know it's a big step, but I really want to pursue dance. It's my passion,' I said, my voice shaking a little.

My uncle sat down and looked at me kindly. 'I understand, dear,' he said. 'I know your father can be very strict, but he just wants you to have a secure future.' I felt a spark of hope—maybe my uncle could help change my father's mind.

My uncle reassured me with a warm smile. 'Manisha, pursuing your passion is important. If you truly believe in your dreams, you should follow them. I'll talk to your father and try to help him understand,' he promised. I felt a deep gratitude: my uncle's support felt like a lifeline.

The following days were filled with both anxiety optimism. My uncle took it upon himself to engage my father in conversation, and so help him understand my aspirations. These dialogues were frequently intense; but gradually, my father's stance began to shift. Although he remained unconvinced about my choice, he ultimately agreed to allow me to pursue it. However, he imposed one condition: if my plans fell through, I would need to come back and secure a stable job.

I felt relieved. It wasn't a perfect outcome, but it was a chance, an opportunity to pursue my passion and see where it could lead. I thanked my father, my mother and my uncle for their support and understanding. Though I knew the path ahead would be difficult, I was ready to walk it with determination.

6

The Letter Under the Pillow

Kolkata had made a significant impact on me long before I even spoke with Priyanka. While I was in my twelfth grade, I visited this bustling city to attend the wedding of a relative. The dynamic spirit and deep cultural heritage of Kolkata attracted me; they remain indelible in my memory. The wedding provided the perfect backdrop for a serendipitous encounter that I would not forget.

As I navigated through the crowd, I accidentally bumped into a stranger.

'Oh! I'm sorry,' I exclaimed, embarrassment colouring my cheeks.

The stranger, a tall man with a friendly smile, replied warmly, 'No problem at all.'

'I'm Steve, and you are?'

'Manisha,' I introduced myself, my curiosity sparked.

It wasn't often I met someone with such an intriguing name.

'Steve?' I echoed, puzzled.

'*Yeh kya maajra hai*? That doesn't sound like a typical Indian name, and you don't seem like a foreigner. What's the story behind it?' Steve let out a soft chuckle: 'I work at a BPO centre here in Kolkata,' he explained, 'and I chose this name because I like it and often interact with clients from abroad. It just felt appropriate. And what about you? What do you do?' My eyes sparkled as I replied, 'I'm a dancer. Dancing is my passion, and I aspire to become a professional dancer one day.' Steve's expression brightened with interest. 'That's wonderful! Are you here with the bride's family or the groom's?' he asked. I smiled and replied, 'The groom's side. And you?' He laughed again, 'The groom's side as well! What a coincidence!'

The conversation flowed effortlessly; we spent hours sharing our thoughts, dreams and experiences. Eventually, Steve said, 'It's getting late; I should head out. But remember, if you ever need anything, don't hesitate to reach out.' We exchanged contact numbers, promising to keep in touch. I then returned to Munger to finish my exams.

My mind, however, kept drifting back to Kolkata. Around this time, I called Priyanka, and that conversation played a crucial role in shaping my big decision.

Travel Preparations

Examinations had finally come to an end, and with Baba's blessing, everything was in place for me to move to Kolkata. A surge of joy filled my heart as my family began to organize the move. As the plans unfolded, I felt conflicting emotions; the thought of living away from home for the first time, especially on my own, was both thrilling and daunting. My family had always been my support system, and the idea of leaving them behind was heart-wrenching. To ease my transition, my mother chose to accompany me to Kolkata. This decision not only bolstered my confidence but also reassured my family, who knew that I would have her to ensure my safety and well-being during this significant move.

My most beloved corner of my room was undoubtedly my bed, where my treasured pillow lay. It was upon that pillow that I envisioned my dreams, cried over trials and revelled in my happiness. Each feeling I felt had a companion in that pillow; it was a profoundly significant object in my life. In a reflective moment, I had an idea: I would write a heartfelt letter to my family. In it, I aimed to appreciate them and express my gratitude for their steadfast support. As I wrote, my hands began to shake and my eyes filled with tears. Once the letter was complete, I carefully tucked it beneath my pillow, asking my sister to share it with the family later.

The day arrived at last, and my mother and I got ready to set off for Kolkata. The farewell was bittersweet: I felt many emotions, but they all gave way to a strong sense of resolve. I had already reached out to Steve and Priyanka to let them know about our imminent arrival in the city. Upon our arrival, we were greeted by Steve and Priyanka; soon after, we made ourselves comfortable in Priyanka's room. A few days later, once I had acclimatized to my new surroundings, my mother made the journey back to Jamalpur. This signalled the start of my solo adventure.

Steve played a crucial role in helping me navigate the city. He assisted me in finding dance classes, researching auditions and making valuable connections. My daily routine was demanding—I balanced my chores with intense dance practice and frequent auditions. Despite this hectic schedule and the difficulties of urban commuting, my unwavering determination kept me focused on my dreams and committed to my goals.

Kolkata presented a vibrant tapestry of cultures and endless opportunities; I plunged into its dynamic dance scene, with Steve guiding me through this circuit. He attended auditions and events with me, often standing in long lines, handling paperwork and managing logistics. His kindness and generosity made him a cherished friend and confidant.

My early days in Kolkata were a series of auditions, rehearsals and performances. I quickly discovered that the road to becoming a professional dancer was difficult—the competition was fierce, and the industry could be unforgiving. Yet, I remained resolute, determined to both dance and make my family proud.

This was also a period of immense personal growth. I learned about the complexities of a new city, how to manage my finances and deal with the emotional ups and downs that came with pursuing this career. My relationship with Steve deepened, evolving into a close friendship based on mutual respect and support.

Steve deeply admired my grit and often marvelled at my ability to remain positive despite the many obstacles I encountered. He was always ready with a listening ear and a helping hand whenever I needed it. Our friendship grew into a source of strength for both of us; such is the transformative power of genuine human connection.

In the midst of the chaos of auditions and rehearsals, Priyanka and I, unfortunately, found ourselves at odds; a rift grew and led us to part ways. This unexpected change meant I had to find a new place to live, one that fit my budget and offered a fresh start.

Steve, ever the supportive friend, jumped in to help. He took the time to help me search for a new, affordable apartment, easing the stress of moving and letting me concentrate on my dance career. His assistance was more than practical; it was a reminder that I wasn't alone, even as my world shifted around me. Steve's steadfast help during this challenging transition allowed me to ease into my new circumstances with a sense of stability.

In moments of loneliness, I turned to my grandmother for comfort, pouring my heart out in letters. These letters became more than just a way to communicate; they were my lifeline, a means of sharing my deepest fears and triumphs. Writing them helped me process my emotions and feel connected to home.

Dadi, always a pillar of strength to me, responded with letters full of wisdom and affection. She didn't just offer advice; she shared stories from her own life, tales of overcoming difficulties and finding hope in hard times. Her words brought me both solace and inspiration from afar.

My grandmother's encouragement and thoughtful reflections helped me stay grounded. Each letter was a reminder of her constant belief in me, reinforcing my confidence as I continued on the demanding path of my dance career. The bond forged through these letters was a testament to the power of family and of love.

I kept the letters tucked under my pillow, reading them each night before bed. The comfort and motivation I found in those words recharged me for the next day. It was a profound and unexplainable feeling of comfort and strength that helped me face each new challenge with renewed energy.

Daring to dream on a grand scale requires a willingness to make sacrifices. Your background is irrelevant; what truly matters is your self-belief and your readiness to confront challenges directly. Embrace the obstacles that come your way, for they are stepping stones on your journey. With determination and resilience, success will undoubtedly find its way to you.

7

Undeterred: Facing Unknown Obstacles with Courage

In the hustle and bustle of city life, I had crafted a routine around chasing my dreams. I attended many rehearsals and auditions, all driven by a singular goal, to make it big in the world of dance. One day, an unexpected opportunity came my way. A coordinator from my dance class offered me a chance to perform in a remote town called Chhapra, with the promise of Rs 500 a day. Though hesitant, I decided to take the plunge, hoping it would be the break I needed.

The journey to the village was long and exhausting. When I finally arrived, I found the place was isolated, and the living conditions were rough. The dancers, including myself, were crammed into a tiny room, with no proper bathroom facilities. While the other dancers seemed to take it all in stride, quickly preparing for their performance in their flashy outfits and heavy make-up, I felt a growing sense of discomfort.

The performance was set to take place on a truck, with the audience surrounding us. The whole situation felt overwhelming and strange. My gut feeling told me that something was wrong; I began to feel more and more anxious.

When I voiced my concerns to the coordinator, he was rude and dismissive. He warned me that if I decided to leave, he wouldn't be responsible for my safety in this isolated area. His words only heightened my anxiety, and I felt I had to act. Summoning all my courage, I decided to leave.

Fearful but determined, I set out on foot through the dense, unfamiliar terrain. The path was difficult and the surroundings unnerving, but I pushed on, driven by the need to escape. After a gruelling journey, I finally reached a highway and was able to find my way back to Kolkata.

The experience was frightening and disheartening and left me shaken. I took some time to recover, but I refused to let this setback discourage me. My resolve to succeed remained strong. I continued to hope that my hard work would eventually pay off. The ordeal had been a tough lesson, but it only strengthened my belief in myself and my courage. I now understood that the road would be tough and at times treacherous, and I had to keep my wits around.

One of my early breaks came when I was cast as a background dancer for a prominent show in Bhagalpur. This was my chance to showcase my talents and gain valuable exposure in the dance world.

However, the experience turned out to be far from ideal. The conditions were tough there too, and the treatment of the dancers was far from professional. I faced unwelcome advances and uncomfortable situations, a harsh reality to suffer through.

Despite these challenges, I continued to audition and search for better opportunities, my determination undimmed. These efforts eventually paid off when I was offered a chance to perform at an exhibition show in Digha. The coordinator promised a more professional environment, and I decided to take the risk.

The atmosphere at the exhibition was electric, the stage was impressive and the audience's enthusiasm was palpable. As I prepared backstage with the other dancers, I could feel the difference. The environment was far more organized and the treatment respectful, compared to my previous experiences. The dressing rooms were well-equipped, and the costumes were elegant and flattering.

When the performance began, I felt a familiar joy. The music enveloped me, and I moved gracefully, my body fully in tune with its rhythm and emotion. The applause from the audience at the end of the performance was a sweet affirmation of my hard work and talent.

As I changed back into my regular clothes after the show, I couldn't help but smile. Despite the setbacks I had faced, moments like this made it all worthwhile. I felt a deep sense of fulfilment and pride in what I had achieved, knowing that my hard work had led me to this rewarding experience.

As the months passed, I started gaining recognition in the dance community by participating in more shows and competitions. My unique style and expressive performances caught the attention of choreographers and directors, opening doors to more significant opportunities.

The Dance Reality Show

In 2015, I landed an audition for the fifth season of *Dance India Dance*, one of India's most prestigious dance competition shows. This was a crucial milestone in my journey, offering the recognition I had longed for in the entertainment industry.

The day of the audition arrived. While many competitors opted for Western-style dance attire, I decided to stay true to my roots. I meticulously packed my favourite sari and blouse, eager to showcase my talent while honouring my cultural heritage.

The audition process in Kolkata was gruelling, consisting of three rounds before the televised segment of the competition. As I looked at the long line of hopeful dancers, I felt the pressure. Fortunately, my old friend Steve stepped in to help, holding my place in line so I could focus on last-minute practice and mental preparation.

While waiting for my turn, I observed my competition with a mix of awe and apprehension. Many of the dancers were trained by renowned choreographers like Ganesh

Acharya and Terence Lewis, their polished moves a testament to years of rigorous training. For a moment, self-doubt crept in—I questioned myself, uncertain whether my passion and dedication could match their technical skill.

But I was not one to give in easily. I took a deep breath, reminding myself of the countless hours I had invested in honing my craft, and stepped onto the stage when my name was called, ready to give it my all.

As the music started, I lost myself in the rhythm. My movements embodied both grace and strength, each step narrating the story of my journey from a small village to this prestigious stage. The judges watched intently, their expressions unreadable as I poured my heart into every beat.

In those moments, I gave everything I had, transforming my nerves into a powerful performance that spoke volumes about my dedication and passion.

As the music faded, I stood breathless, my heart racing as I awaited the judges' decision. To my immense joy and relief, I was selected for the second round. The judges not only praised my performance but also commended my choice of attire. When asked why I chose to dance in a sari, my response was heartfelt and sincere.

'This is what I feel most comfortable in. It's what everyone wears in my village. It allows me to express my love for dance while honouring my cultural roots; to me, it's a way of promoting Indian culture through my art.'

Delighted with my success, I approached the second round with even more enthusiasm. My performance once again impressed the judges, earning me a coveted spot in the third and final round of the Kolkata auditions.

Steve's Support

As I waited for my turn in the final round, that old anxiety began to resurface. I found myself wondering if I truly had what it took to compete at this level. The fear of failing and disappointing my family loomed in my mind.

Sensing my distress, Steve approached me with a glass of water and comforting words. 'Manisha,' he said gently, 'don't let fear hold you back. You have incredible talent and a passion for dance that sets you apart. Remember, every great dancer has faced setbacks. It's how you respond to them that truly matters.'

Steve's words struck a deep chord with me, helping to restore my confidence. When my name was finally called, I took a deep breath and stepped onto the stage, ready to give it my all.

My performance once again showcased my skill and dedication. My movements flowed effortlessly, each gesture infused with emotion. As I finished, the audience erupted in applause, and I saw the impressed looks on the judges' faces.

The wait for the results felt like an eternity, but finally, the moment of truth arrived. When I heard that I had qualified for the TV round of *Dance India Dance*, I could hardly believe it. Overwhelmed with elation, I embraced Steve tightly, tears of joy streaming down my face.

'I couldn't have done this without your support,' I said, my voice choking with gratitude. 'Thank you for believing in me.'

Steve smiled warmly. 'I'm just glad I could help. You've earned this, Manisha. Best of luck for what lies ahead!'

With the TV round approaching, my dream of performing in Mumbai, the heart of India's entertainment industry, was on the verge of coming true. I immediately called my father to share the incredible news.

The Reaction

I was thrilled to inform my father that I had qualified for the TV round of *Dance India Dance*, but my father's reaction was not what I had hoped for. He was worried about sending me to Mumbai, so far from home, especially given his inability to take time off work. Disheartened by his hesitation, I tried to reach my sister Sarika, but she wasn't home.

Nonetheless, I threw myself into preparing for my performance. When Sarika called back later that day, I shared the exciting news. Unlike our father, she was ecstatic and immediately offered to help persuade him to support my journey.

Sarika worked tirelessly at this, stressing the importance of this rare opportunity for me. 'Papa,' she argued, 'this is her chance to shine on a national stage. We need to support her dreams.'

Sarika's passionate plea eventually made our father change his mind. He agreed to accompany me to Mumbai. As we set off on our journey, I reflected on how far I had come. The support from my father and sister had been crucial to this progress.

You know that moment when your dreams seem *so close*, yet something keeps holding you back? I've been there—standing in front of the mirror, heart racing, wondering if I was good enough to call myself a dancer.

Throughout my journey, I have often wrestled with feelings of self-doubt, pondering whether I genuinely embody the traits required to call myself a dancer. Despite these moments, my determination to succeed has remained strong. The key lies in relentless effort and perseverance; if you commit yourself to your aspirations and push through the challenges, you will ultimately reach your destination. Life presents us with numerous opportunities—it's essential to recognize and seize them.

8

Mumbai: The City of Dreams

News of my achievement quickly spread through Munger, filling the villagers with pride. For many, the idea of someone from our small town appearing on national television seemed almost unbelievable. Their fervour and good wishes gave me a growing sense of purpose.

Arriving in Mumbai was a sensory overload for me. The city's towering skyscrapers, diverse people and fast-paced lifestyle were a stark contrast to the quiet streets of Munger. As we made our way to my uncle's home, where we would be staying, my eyes darted around, taking in the sights and sounds of this vibrant metropolis.

My aunt and uncle welcomed us warmly, prepared a hearty breakfast for us and offered their enthusiastic support. My uncle, who had lived in Mumbai for years, offered to guide us to the audition venue, his local knowledge proving invaluable.

The day of the TV round audition arrived, and I was awestruck by the massive studios and the palpable buzz in the air. Meeting the judges in person felt surreal; I was also surprised to find that many people recognized me from the previous rounds. Some even came up to offer words of encouragement; these were both comforting and slightly overwhelming.

As I waited with my father and sister, my old insecurities resurfaced. The other contestants seemed so polished and professional, their years of formal training evident in every movement. I felt the weight of my rural background more than ever, wondering if I truly belonged on this grand stage.

Sarika, noticing the worry on my face, asked, 'What's wrong? You look troubled.'

I hesitated before admitting, 'Sarika, do you think I can compete with these professionally trained dancers? They seem so far ahead of me.'

Before Sarika could respond, our father spoke up, his voice firm yet comforting: 'Manisha, your talent is extraordinary and comes from a place of genuine passion. That's something no amount of training can replicate. Don't compare yourself to others. Focus on doing your best and let your love for dance shine through.'

His unexpected, heartfelt words brought tears to my eyes. I could only nod in response.

When my name was called, I stepped onto the stage with renewed determination. As the music began, I let go of my doubts and fears, allowing my body to move with the rhythm. My performance was a perfect blend of technical skill and raw emotion, and captivated both the judges and the audience.

As the final notes faded, I was met with thunderous applause. The judges' faces lit up with approval, and for a moment, I allowed herself to believe that my dreams were truly within reach.

Elimination

However, fate had other plans. Despite my impressive performance and the judges' praise, I was eliminated in the fourth round. The news hit me like a physical blow, leaving me heartbroken. All my hopes and dreams seemed to have crumbled in an instant, and I found myself questioning everything I had worked so hard for.

The journey back to Munger was sombre. My mind raced with thoughts of what people would say and how I had let everyone down. Yet, I clung to the memory of how far I had come, of the pride I had seen in my neighbours' eyes when I left for Mumbai.

Upon returning home, I was surprised to find the villagers still brimming with pride and joy. They showered me with congratulations, eager to hear about my experiences in the big city. Their genuine happiness for my accomplishments, regardless of the outcome, helped soothe some of my disappointment.

In the days that followed, I tried to find solace in helping with household chores and continuing my dance practice. The discipline I had developed in Kolkata served me well during this difficult time.

Mother's Comfort

Seeking comfort and guidance, Sarika and I decided to visit our mother in Jamalpur. The reunion was emotional, with our mother hugging us tightly and expressing her pride in my achievements. However, I couldn't hold back my feelings of failure any longer.

'I've let everyone down,' I confessed, tears flowing from my eyes. 'All those years in Kolkata, and I have nothing to show for it.'

My mother's response was gentle but firm. 'You haven't let anyone down, Manisha. You've made us all proud. Every experience teaches us something valuable, helping us grow and become stronger.'

Seeing that I needed more comforting, my mother decided to share a story we had heard before. 'Let me tell you about the brave princess,' she began, drawing our attention.

'Once upon a time, there was a courageous princess named Aradhya. She lived in a grand palace but dreamed of becoming a warrior like her father. Despite disapproval from the palace guards and the court, she practised secretly every night, honing her sword skills.

'One day, a neighbouring kingdom declared war. The palace was thrown into chaos, and the king was injured in battle. With no one else to lead, Aradhya took up her father's sword and led the soldiers. Despite the odds, she fought valiantly and they emerged victorious.

'The lesson, my dear Manisha, is that Aradhya didn't let fear stop her. She believed in herself and her abilities, just as you must believe in yourself. Your journey isn't limited by a single setback. There are many paths ahead for you to explore.'

I listened closely, feeling uplifted by my mother's words. 'You've always been my guiding light, Maa,' I said, wiping away my tears. 'I promise I won't stop believing in myself. I'll face whatever comes my way, knowing that one day, I'll secure my dreams.'

My mother smiled warmly. 'That's the spirit, my brave girl. Remember, I'm always here for you. No matter the obstacles, confront them and keep moving forward.'

I also shared with my mother how supportive my father had been during the *Dance India Dance* auditions. My mother was pleasantly surprised and delighted. 'I would have never expected that from your father,' she admitted. 'I'm so glad he's coming around. I hope he continues to encourage your dreams.'

As Sarika and I prepared to return to Munger, we were happy again. Despite this, I still grappled with conflicting feelings. I yearned to pursue my passion fully, but knew that my family expectations differed.

Passion for Dance

One evening, as I sat lost in thought on the veranda, my grandmother approached me. 'Now that you've completed your graduation, it's time to think seriously about your future,' she said, her tone carrying a serious note.

I took a deep breath before responding. 'Yes, Dadi, I understand. But I want to pursue my passion for dance. It brings me so much happiness and satisfaction.'

My grandmother's expression hardened slightly. 'Manisha, you know our family is traditional. Our values and customs are more important than your dance. Besides, dance cannot build a stable career.'

Hoping to find some middle ground, I replied gently, 'Dadi, I understand your concerns and respect our family traditions. But I believe we can honour our values while still pursuing our dreams.'

My grandmother said nothing more, simply retreating to her room, leaving me to ponder how I could reconcile my ambitions with what my family expected of me.

As days turned into weeks, I continued to practise tirelessly, finding ways to pursue my art even within the confines of Munger. My dedication had redoubled.

'Munger ki Beti' Is Born

Then, a month after my return from Mumbai, something unexpected happened. The episode featuring my *Dance India Dance* performance was finally aired on television. To my amazement, it garnered widespread popularity and admiration from viewers across the country. Suddenly, I found myself thrust into the spotlight. My social media accounts were flooded with new followers, likes and messages of support. People began calling me 'Munger ki Beti'—the daughter of Munger—with pride and affection.

This fresh recognition reignited my confidence and strengthened my will to pursue my passion for dance. In the streets of Munger, locals celebrated their hometown hero.

Just when I thought things couldn't get any more extraordinary, a social media post titled 'Manisha Rani *ne dikhaye master* Punit *ko apne dance ke jalwe*' (Manisha Rani showcases her dance prowess to master Punit) went viral. The video spread like wildfire across various platforms, catching the attention of several prominent figures in the dance industry.

As I basked in the joy of my recent successes, I received a life-changing phone call. The caller, Rajan, introduced himself as a professional dancer who ran a dance academy. He explained that he had been following my journey since my *Dance India Dance* audition and was deeply impressed by my raw talent and dedication.

Rajan shared exciting news: he was launching a dance troupe for the upcoming season of *India's Got Talent*, one of the country's most popular talent shows, and he wanted me to be a part of it. He recognized my potential to shine on an even bigger stage.

I could hardly believe what I was hearing. The chance to participate in *India's Got Talent* felt like a dream come true. My heart raced as I realized my dance journey was about to reach new heights.

Before this stage, I decided to return to Kolkata for intensive preparation. However, upon arriving in the city, I faced an immediate challenge—I had nowhere to stay.

As I began my search for affordable accommodation, Rajan stepped in to assist. He contacted a warm-hearted woman connected with his dance academy, who agreed to provide me with temporary lodging. The woman had a daughter close to my age, and I quickly became a part of their household, helping with daily chores as a token of my appreciation.

Life in Kolkata was again hectic. My days started at 5.30 a.m., when I helped my host with her tasks before rushing to the dance academy for rigorous rehearsals. I pushed my body to its limits, preparing tirelessly for *India's Got Talent*. Evenings were spent searching for a permanent place to stay, as I was needed to become independent.

The demanding schedule took its toll, but my dream of succeeding on *India's Got Talent* kept me motivated. I drew strength from my mother's encouraging words and the support of my family back in Munger.

After weeks of searching, I finally found a small, one-room apartment with a modest kitchen and bathroom. The rent was Rs 3000, a significant amount for me, but I saw it as an investment in my future. Having my own place allowed me to focus entirely on preparing for the show without feeling like a burden on my generous hosts. I shared my news with Rajan and the kind woman who had sheltered me, expressing my heartfelt gratitude.

With my new apartment, I established a new routine. My mornings started with a simple breakfast made in the tiny kitchen, followed by intense practice sessions at the academy. In the evenings, I would perfect my routines in the privacy of my apartment. This tiny space became a sanctuary where I could fully express myself through dance.

Despite the long hours and physical strain, my spirits remained high. Each day brought new lessons as I worked with my fellow dancers in Rajan's troupe. Our chemistry grew stronger each week, and this increasing chemistry promised to create a brilliant performance for the upcoming show.

The key takeaway is to not allow your fears to hold you back. Avoid the trap of comparing your progress to that of others. Instead, concentrate on giving your utmost effort and have faith in your own abilities.

Regardless of the obstacles you face, face them head-on and continue to progress. Remember, a single moment does not determine the entirety of your journey. There are countless avenues waiting for you to discover and pursue. Never give up.

9

The Breakthrough

India's Got Talent

As the audition for *India's Got Talent* drew near, familiar insecurities returned to haunt me. The memory of my previous elimination from *Dance India Dance* lingered in my mind, fuelling my worry that I might face a similar fate once again. In the quiet hours of the night, after countless hours of relentless practice, I often caught myself gazing into the mirror, racked with self-doubt and wondering if I truly had what it took to shine on such a prestigious platform. In these moments, I would often find peace by shutting my eyes and revisiting the tale of Princess Aradhya, as recounted lovingly by my mother. This narrative became a source of strength for me: it was a reminder that genuine bravery lies in confronting and enduring one's fears. With each recollection, I transformed my uncertainties into a powerful drive to push forward.

As the troupe's routines took shape, Rajan noticed my exceptional dedication and natural talent. He involved me more in the creative process, valuing my inputs and encouraging me to explore my artistic vision. This vote of confidence boosted my self-esteem and helped me tap into creative reserves I didn't know I had. One evening, after a particularly gruelling rehearsal, Rajan pulled me aside.

'You've come a long way since I first saw you,' he said with pride. 'Your growth as a dancer and as a person has been remarkable. I believe *India's Got Talent* will be your moment to truly shine.'

I was deeply touched by his words. 'Thank you, sir,' I replied, my voice thick with emotion. 'I'm giving this everything I have. I want to make you, my family and Munger proud.'

Rajan smiled warmly. 'You already have, Manisha. Now it's time to show the rest of India what you're capable of.'

As the day of the audition drew near, the atmosphere at the dance academy grew electric. The dancers put countless hours into refining their routine, meticulously attending to every aspect, from their costumes to the nuances of their facial expressions. I threw myself into the preparations, eager to ensure that every element was flawless and that no detail was overlooked. With the audition on the following day, I found myself perched on my bed, cradling my phone as I engaged in a heartfelt conversation with my family back in Munger. Their supportive words wrapped around me like a warm blanket, filling me with love and motivation. In the soft glow of the room, I was surrounded by treasured photographs and keepsakes, each one a reminder of my journey.

I reflected on the distance I had travelled and the experiences that had shaped me into who I am today. From dancing at village festivals to preparing for one of India's biggest stages, my journey had been filled with highs and lows. Yet my passion for dance had been a constant guide. As I drifted off to sleep, my dreams were filled with vibrant colours and rhythmic beats, envisioning myself dancing on the stage.

On the morning of the audition, the day was bright and clear, as if the universe itself was cheering for me and my fellow dancers. At the academy, Rajan gathered us for a final pep talk, his face expressing both seriousness and encouragement.

'Remember why we're here,' he said, his voice steady. 'We're not just dancers; we're storytellers. Today, we get to share our passion and art with the entire country. No matter what happens, I'm proud of each one of you. Let's give the performance of our lives!'

We made our way to the audition venue. The bustling streets of Kolkata seemed to blur as I mentally rehearsed our routine. Arriving at the studio, the sight of bright lights, cameras and the famous judges' panel took my breath away. But as I took my place on stage with my troupe, I felt a calm sense of belonging. As the music began, I let go of all my doubts and fears, immersing myself in the dance. My movements married rhythm, emotion and technical skill.

The performance felt like it passed in an instant. As the final notes played and the troupe struck their closing pose, the studio erupted in applause. I awaited the judges' verdict, barely able to breathe.

The first judge, visibly moved, spoke, 'That was breathtaking. The way you moved together, telling a story through dance—it was truly magical.'

The second judge nodded, her gaze fixed on me. 'I was particularly struck by the young lady in the centre. There's a raw passion in your performance that's impossible to ignore. You dance as if your soul depends on it.'

As the judges continued their praise, my eyes filled with tears of joy. While Rajan stepped forward to hear the judges' decision, the entire troupe awaited expectantly. The head judge's voice rang out clearly, 'We'd be honoured to have you compete in the next round of *India's Got Talent*!'

The studio burst into cheers, and I was enveloped in a group hug with my fellow dancers. As we celebrated, I caught Rajan's eye. His proud smile conveyed everything words could not.

The initial three rounds of *India's Got Talent* were incredibly smooth for our group. Our performances received immense acclaim and a flood of votes, and I noticed that many, particularly those new to the dance scene, were drawn to my abilities. During the fourth round, our troupe put on a remarkable show that impressed the judges and the audience alike. We felt a strong sense of assurance that this performance would guarantee our advancement to the next stage of the competition.

However, fate had other plans: the entire team was eliminated from the competition.

The news was devastating, especially for me. It felt like I was reliving the heartbreak from my previous setback. Overwhelmed and uncertain about my future, I struggled to process the outcome. I managed to inform my parents about the results, and they suggested I return to Munger.

Picture Abhi Baki Hai

In 2018, TikTok was revolutionizing the world of social media. Yet, I was initially hesitant to join the platform. As I observed friends and acquaintances rising to fame through their TikTok content, my intrigue grew, and I ultimately decided to explore the app for myself. I started off by producing straightforward lip-sync videos, utilizing basic gear and creatively employing what resources I had at my disposal. I carefully chose audio clips and costumes to elevate my content, capturing everything on my phone in portrait orientation. By reaching out to friends for tips,

I discovered ways to optimize my limited resources and develop my video-making skills.

As I explored the world of content creation further, it became increasingly clear that I needed to upgrade my smartphone in order to enhance the quality of my videos. After conducting more research, I discovered that the ideal phone for my purposes was unfortunately out of my financial reach. However, with a commitment to my future in mind, I made the decision to acquire the phone through an EMI plan, amounting to Rs 26,000. This financial obligation was considerable, but to me, it was an essential investment in my journey toward success. In addition to the phone, a tripod was also necessary to ensure my shots were stable—I had previously struggled with makeshift setups that often resulted in shaky footage. To ensure that my videos looked as professional as possible, I also purchased a black curtain from a local market, which I used to conceal the unappealing brick wall in my filming space. Each of these purchases, while seemingly modest on their own, symbolized a significant leap forward in my quest to turn my dreams into reality.

For the next eight to nine months, I immersed myself completely in creating content for TikTok. I committed to a daily practice routine, continuously honing my abilities and experimenting with fresh concepts. Every day, at 10 a.m. in the morning, I would get dressed and make my way to the terrace, where I would craft new videos until 6 in the evening.

Then, one afternoon, my family returned home earlier than expected and discovered my set-up. There was a rather severe and dismissive reaction from them; '*Inn sab chizo se kuch nahi hota hai, sab bekar ki baatein hain,*' they said. I was deeply hurt by their words—was I on the right path? Yet, despite this disapproval, I held on to the belief that TikTok could lead me to something greater.

Handling Popularity

After nine months of perfecting my lip-syncing, I took a bold step and recorded a video with my own audio.

The instant I hit the publish button, I felt anxious. But, to my astonishment, the video exploded in popularity almost immediately, amassing a million views within just one night. The barrage of notifications that followed was new to me and a bit daunting, yet it also filled me with a sense of exhilaration. This unexpected success unveiled a realm of opportunities I had never considered before. Fuelled by this momentum, I dove into creating a variety of content, eager to stretch my creative limits. My videos began to not only entertain but also inspire others—people would incorporate my audio into their own projects. Witnessing this ripple effect was nothing short of surreal.

I began attending events in Delhi, meeting fellow creators and fans, which further validated my decision.

As my TikTok presence grew, I began to explore other online platforms to expand my reach.

Instagram, TV Show and Mumbai!

In 2019, I redirected my attention towards Instagram, then already a burgeoning social media platform that was drawing millions of users. At the time, I had no inkling that this would pave the way towards a remarkable turning point in my professional life. That very year, I received an unforeseen phone call from the producers of the popular television show, *Gudiya Hamari Sabhi Pe Bhari*, airing on &TV; they extended an offer for me to portray a character who would befriend the lead. I eagerly shared this thrilling news with my family; now fully supportive of my aspirations, they agreed to travel with me to Mumbai for the auditions. Upon arriving, I faced a reality check: the pay was just Rs 2500 per day, far below what I needed to cover my expenses in Mumbai. Despite the low pay, my family and I decided to accept the offer, seeing it as a crucial step towards my goals.

With my father's reluctant blessing, I moved to Mumbai to be with my sister Sarika, who was working in the city. We settled into a modest room with two other girls. As I lay in bed one night, I voiced my worries to Sarika, who reassured me with warmth.

'You've come so far already,' Sarika said, placing a comforting hand on my shoulder. 'Remember your self-worth, the resourcefulness you've shown so far. You'll manage, just trust yourself.'

Buoyed by her words, I was, now ready to face whatever lay ahead on *Gudiya Hamari Sabhi Pe Bhari*.

I had to adapt quickly to the rigorous filming schedule of the show. The long days, that stretched to twelve, even thirteen hours each day, were a significant shift from the freedom I had enjoyed on social media. Still, I kept myself motivated with the belief that I needed to prove my worth. I portrayed the best friend of the lead character; this character was also a social media influencer, allowed me to draw from my own experiences and make my performance more authentic. One particularly unforgettable moment in the script had my character hilariously barging into a room and declaring, '*Ye aa gaye hai hum apni angrezi class me, or ye hai humari friend Gudiya aur aaj hum milne wale hai Gudiya ke vaha do handsome ladko se. Phir hum dekhenge ki kaun hai humara boyfriend banne ke layak.*' (Here we are in our English class, and this is our friend Gudiya. Today we're going to meet two handsome boys there. Then we'll see who is worthy of being our boyfriend.)

My genuine portrayal impressed the creators and deepened my connection with viewers, who recognized my real-life experiences on screen.

Even with the demanding television schedule, I continued to create content for TikTok. Many nights found me filming videos so late that dinner would be pushed back. Sarika would patiently wait for me, prepare my dinner and always remind me that I had her backing. Although the path was fraught with sacrifices, my hard work eventually bore fruit. The uplifting responses from my online followers motivated me to persist with both the TV show and my digital endeavours.

Balancing both worlds, I would often reflect on my progress from Munger to Mumbai. Despite the pressure and occasional anxiety from camera scrutiny, the support from my family and friends, including Steve, helped me stay focused.

Every performance presented an opportunity for growth, and I constantly reminded myself: 'Each performance enhances my skills.' I committed wholeheartedly to my character in the TV series, putting in extensive hours from December 2019 through March 2020. Unfortunately, as the global pandemic began to unfold, the show was abruptly taken off the air on 15 March, putting a sudden end to my television debut. The introduction of the lockdown in India on 22 March ushered in a daunting new reality, leaving Sarika and me very concerned about what the future held. I received little reassurance from the producer. As weeks turned into months with no end to the lockdown in sight, the show was ultimately cancelled, leaving me feeling lost and disheartened.

During the initial months of the pandemic, the once-vibrant city of Mumbai felt desolate. I called Steve, who advised me to expand my online presence. But the reality of the situation was tough. With no immediate opportunities and the lockdown dragging on, I decided to return to Munger in June.

Travelling during the lockdown was very difficult. Watching Mumbai's skyline recede from the train window, I felt a sense of resignation, wondering when or if I would return to chase my dreams.

TikTok Ban

Amid the turmoil of the COVID-19 pandemic, I faced an unexpected reverse. The Indian government banned fifty-nine Chinese apps, including TikTok, due to concerns over national security. TikTok, a crucial platform for my career, one with over 200 million users in India, was now inaccessible, leaving me feeling disheartened. The sudden ban seemed like a personal setback. Confused and worried, I turned to Sarika yet again for advice.

'Didi, TikTok has been banned. What do I do now?' I asked in a tentative voice.

Sarika suggested concentrating my efforts on other platforms, such as Instagram or YouTube. Taking her advice, I shifted my focus to Instagram's Reels, a similar short-form video feature. Although the transition held challenges—different algorithms, varied audience expectations and starting from scratch—I took it on. Slowly but surely, my hard work began to pay off. My follower count grew, and I started earning between Rs 5000 and Rs 10,000 per month from my content. It wasn't a fortune, but it marked a promising new beginning.

Sharing my success with my family, I said, 'It's a start. I'm making some money from my videos.' My relieved family encouraged me to keep pursuing my passion. The ban on TikTok had turned into an opportunity for growth and adaptation for me.

Mumbai Meri Jaan

The support of my family was a pillar of strength for me in those tough times. As 2020 ended and 2021 began, I decided to return to Mumbai.

'No more relying on others,' I told my family. 'This time, I'll prove myself.'

Packing my bags, I reassured myself aloud, 'I can do this. Mumbai is where my dreams can come true. This is my chance to shine.'

Despite lingering feelings of uncertainty, I focused on staying positive. With my bags packed and my optimism high, I set off for Mumbai once again. My father accompanied me, since my elder sister had recently got married. In Mumbai, I rented a room near Heera Panna, sharing it with four other girls who soon became friends with me. I immersed myself in my work, regularly posting content on YouTube and MX TakaTak, a new short-video platform that emerged after TikTok's ban. My efforts began to pay off, and I started earning around Rs 30,000 per month from my videos. This financial independence was a significant milestone, proving that my goals were within reach.

To further hone my skills, I enrolled in advanced dance classes. This, to me, was an act of investing in my future; it would stand out in the competitive content creation world. I attended numerous auditions, as I had in Kolkata, viewing each one as a chance to learn and to use feedback to continually improve.

Exhausting but Exhilarating

My days were busy from the very start. Mornings started with gruelling dance sessions that pushed me to my limits. The dance studio became a place where the city's chaos faded away, and I could lose myself in music and movement.

The afternoons and evenings found me racing through Mumbai's bustling streets, going from one audition to the next. Every audition was a chance to shine, but not every day ended with a win. Rejections stung, but they were part of the process of growth. On the brighter days, a callback or a kind word from a casting director felt like a small victory, a reminder that I was on the right path.

Nights were for social media—they would run very late, as I'd edit videos, brainstorm new ideas and interact with my growing follower base. It was tiring, but seeing my audience grow and receiving positive feedback boosted me.

Living in Mumbai was a constant balancing act between setbacks and triumphs. The city's fast pace and the fierce competition at every point often felt overwhelming, but I held on tight to my dreams. I reminded myself of how far I had come and kept moving forward.

10

Ek Bihari Sab Par Bhari

As I looked back, I recalled the early days in 2017 when I first dreamt of joining *Bigg Boss*. Back then, I had made a video expressing enthusiasm for the show, my words brimming with hope:

'Hello, *namaste, pranaam* Bigg Boss *aur* Bigg Boss *ki aankh! Hum hai* Manisha Rani, *humari mast hai kahani . . .*'

I tried to send the video to the *Bigg Boss* team, but it never reached them. The disappointment stung but I decided to try again. I made and posted a new video on the 'Celebrity vs Commoner' theme, which caught the attention of an influencer. The praise I received—'You are made for *Bigg Boss*'—filled me with hope.

When the influencer reached out to me with an invitation that promised to bring me closer to *Bigg Boss*, I was over the moon. I hopped into an autorickshaw, my pulse racing as I repeatedly checked my phone, fantasizing about what it would be like to live in the *Bigg Boss* house. However, as I arrived at the hotel where we were supposed to meet, my initial thrill began to wane, replaced by a growing sense of discomfort. The influencer's ambiguous directions and the suggestion to come to a private room raised red flags for me. Trusting my instincts, I firmly requested to meet in a more public setting and left the hotel, disappointed over the situation but also relieved to have avoided it.

Later, I learned from another girl that the individual who had contacted me was merely a driver, and the actual influencer was out of town. I felt utterly deceived. In frustration, I blocked the number and changed my status to 'The world is full of bad people' to reflect my disillusionment. I told my family that I hadn't made the cut for the show, carefully omitting the true details, as I didn't want to burden them with worry. I came to understand this experience as a powerful reminder to listen to my intuition and exercise constant caution. Nonetheless, my aspiration to participate in *Bigg Boss* continued to burn brightly within me. I recognized that the path forward is seldom straightforward, yet armed with the insights I gained and my faith in my abilities, I felt prepared to forge ahead.

A Memory to Cherish

Before I was chosen for *Bigg Boss*, I experienced a significant moment that stands out in my memory. I had the privilege to be part of an audience for an episode of *The Kapil Sharma Show*, which featured the talented Bollywood actor Kartik Aaryan. As a devoted fan of both Kapil Sharma and his entertaining show, I was overjoyed at the prospect of being there, and also believed it could bring me one step closer to my own goals. During the episode, a fun game unfolded where Kartik had to identify his fans based on pre-recorded voice clips. When my voice was played, I seized the moment to convey my admiration, expressing my enthusiasm with heartfelt words, '*Aap humse humari zindagi maang lete, hum khushi khushi de dete, par aapne to humse humara Kartik Aaryan hi chheen liya*' (You could have asked for our lives, and we would have gladly given them to you, but you took away our Kartik Aaryan).

Kartik's face turned a deep shade of crimson as soon as he heard my voice, and he gestured in my direction. The fact that my favourite actor acknowledged me in front of a national audience was utterly exhilarating. This encounter also offered me a tantalizing glimpse of the fame I had always aspired to achieve. It served as a powerful motivator to continue chasing my dreams with full vigour.

The Entry to *Bigg Boss*

My heart raced as I hit 'send' on yet another audition video for *Bigg Boss* in February 2022. Each rejection chipped away at my confidence, but I refused to give up. 'This time,' I told myself, 'this time will be different.'

I approached the task of sharing my videos with much thought, carefully selecting who I would allow to view these snippets of my life, and crafting each one-minute clip to reflect my distinct personality and passions. Despite the labour I poured into these creations, the feedback was often minimal, and the empty assurances I received left me dejected. There were moments when I questioned my own commitment, yet I had to keep going. Then, in January 2023, something happened that transformed everything. Thanks to my tireless networking, a producer from *Bigg Boss* stumbled upon my latest video. When the call came through, informing me of my selection, I was initially in disbelief. After six long years of being an avid follower of the show, I was finally on the brink of my dream. I could already picture myself becoming a household name, gracing magazine covers and appearing on television screens. I felt incredibly fortunate to be invited to compete in *Bigg Boss OTT 2*, something I had longed for.

This new opportunity, while thrilling, was not without its own hurdles. I found myself in a position where I needed to justify my abilities, not just to the organizers of the show but also to myself. The prospect of meeting Salman Khan thrilled me, yet it reminded me of the arduous path I had travelled to reach this point. Memories of my initial foray into this world, marked by a series of rejections, loomed large in my mind. Despite the doubts cast by my family and relatives, I had always managed to summon up the courage to push forward. This time, I made a conscious decision to keep the news of my selection under wraps until I had the contract securely in my possession. As heavily as this secret weighed on me, I believed it was necessary to protect my loved ones from any potential heartache.

The Team

I had quickly become a rising star on Instagram and other platforms. At this early stage of my journey, I had connected with Vishal, a fan who became a trusted friend and guide. Vishal helped me manage my schedules and tackle the complexities of my rapidly growing career.

During this peak of my career, Vishal suggested that I sign with an agency called People Like Us, which was run by his friend Sakett. Trusting Vishal's recommendation, I decided to join this agency to better curate my social media and to address other professional needs; these needs would be crucial as I worked towards reaching the *Bigg Boss* show. I spoke highly of Vishal to Saket, praising the positive impact he had on my professional life.

Thanks to Sakett, this decision paid off when my audition video was selected by the *Bigg Boss* producers.

The Big Day

When the day came to sign my *Bigg Boss* contract, I felt like I was floating. I signed the document with trembling hands, still amazed that my dream was finally coming true. Rushing home, I shared the news with my family. Sarika's face lit up as she hugged me tightly, saying, 'I always knew you could do it. You never gave up!'

Preparations began immediately. I first underwent a detailed medical exam. As I was declared fit for the show, the reality of my situation started to sink in.

Two weeks before the competition, I received the final confirmation call, detailing the rules and regulations. The prospect of being cut off from the outside world was both thrilling and daunting. As I packed my bags, my mind swirled with questions about my fellow contestants, the scrutiny of the cameras and staying true to myself in such a controlled environment. This would definitely be a life-changing experience.

In the *Bigg Boss* House

My time in the *Bigg Boss* house was a rollercoaster ride of emotions and personal development. My genuine nature and relatable charm resonated deeply with the audience, particularly those hailing from small towns who found echoes of their own lives in mine. I built meaningful relationships with several housemates, but also faced significant conflicts with others, which added to the intensity of the experience. Throughout the drama, I remained committed to entertaining the viewers. My charisma and insistence on fairness led to me being dubbed the 'national crush of India', while my popular catchphrase, '*ek Bihari sab pe bhari*,' became a slogan that united my supporters.

The connections made within the *Bigg Boss* house often dissolved once the show concluded and life resumed outside its walls. Several participants displayed a stark contrast between their on-screen personas and their authentic selves when the cameras ceased rolling; they then revealed aspects of their character that had been previously hidden. During quieter moments, I found myself reminiscing about my mother's wise words and the poignant goodbye we shared at the train station. One afternoon, while I was deep in one such reminiscence, a fellow contestant approached me, curious about what was on my mind. Initially reluctant to share my thoughts, I gradually opened up and discussed that touching memory:

'I was at the railway station with my father and my sister Sarika, waiting for the train that would take me to Mumbai. I spotted my mother at the other end of the platform, trying to stay hidden.'

My voice grew soft, and my eyes glistened with tears as I continued, 'I made up an excuse to go see her, but as soon as I reached where she was standing, the train arrived. I had to rush back to board my coach, my heart aching from not having more time with her.'

'But then, a small miracle happened. As the train began to move, my mother carefully approached the train, staying out of my father's and sister's sight. Just as the train started pulling away, my mom reached her hand in through the window,' I recalled, my voice thickening. 'She squeezed my hand and whispered, "Give your best, Manisha. Never forget that I am always proud of you."'

The memory of that emotional moment and my mother's gentle parting words gave me much strength during the hardest days in the *Bigg Boss* house. Each time I felt the weight of the world pressing down on me, those words reminded me of the steadfast love that awaited me back home. As I related this deeply personal experience to my fellow contestant, I found myself contemplating the intricate dynamics of my family.

The separation of my parents had left deep emotional wounds; my father often blaming my mother for their differences. Yet, I had to appreciate my father's strength—how he had faced the task of raising four children alone, striving to fill the void that my mother's absence had created. I thought to myself, 'In a home without a mother, my father had to be both the nurturing figure and the disciplinarian. He carried the weight of our future on his shoulders, doing his best to shield us from feeling the absence of our mother. It must have been an incredibly difficult journey for him.'

I thought back to a recent trip to Abu Dhabi with my parents, the photos from which had been liked by many on social media. The experience had helped bridge some of the distance that had grown between them over the years, as he focused on providing for his children.

'If my mother taught me to fight for my dreams,' I concluded, 'my father taught me the importance of honesty and resoluteness. I owe so much to both of them.'

The Best Is Yet to Come

My experience on *Bigg Boss* was truly life-altering. Finishing as the second runner-up, I won the hearts of countless viewers with my authentic personality and charm. As the show concluded, a plethora of opportunities began to unfold before me. My breakthrough came when I was cast in a music video alongside the famed Tony Kakkar. The track, titled 'Jamnapaar', featured the enchanting vocals of Neha Kakkar, someone I have always looked up to. Standing on the set, ready to shoot, I was awed by this new experience. The chemistry between Tony and me was palpable, and the video went viral almost overnight. Within a matter of days, 'Jamnapaar' amassed millions of views, solidifying my position as an emerging talent in the industry. As I watched the numbers rise, I remembered those nights spent dreaming about *Bigg Boss*; back then, I never foresaw the doors it would open for me. With each achievement, my self-confidence blossomed. I had evolved from a small-town dreamer into a popular presence in the entertainment scene. Looking forward, I realized this was only the start of an extraordinary adventure. My life had undergone a remarkable transformation. The days of struggling and living in a cramped room in Kolkata were behind me. Now, I resided in a lavish apartment in Mumbai, paying a rent of Rs 75,000—a long way from the rent of Rs 1500 for the flat I once shared in Kolkata with my friend Priyanka. I often reminisced about those challenging times when Priyanka and I squeezed into a tiny room with few amenities, scraping together every rupee from our small dance performances, corporate gigs and teaching, each contributing Rs 750 towards our rent.

Now, cruising through Mumbai in my new Mercedes, I marvelled at the contrast between those days and the present. What used to earn me Rs 50,000 now brought in Rs 8,00,000. The rapid success often left me feeling overwhelmed.

Even with the recognition that now came my way, I adhered to my values. I maintained a dedication to philanthropy, as I truly believe that my acts of kindness significantly contribute to my achievements. Generosity had always been something I tried to cultivate in my life; as a young child, I would often divide my birthday money, between treating myself and purchasing necessities for those less fortunate than me. Now, with more money at my disposal, my capacity to assist others expanded tremendously. When I reached 11 million followers on Instagram, I chose to commemorate this milestone by funding the education of eleven girls through a local nonprofit organization. I reflected, 'While I may not have received the best guidance in my early years, I wish to help others have an easier path forward in their lives.'

As I geared up to head back to my hometown for the first time since my spell on *Bigg Boss*, I was naturally very excited. I called my father to ensure he would be there to pick me up from the airport. 'Papa, we should be landing almost on schedule. Can you come to get us?' I asked, my voice tinged with impatience. His response was playful: 'What are you saying, Manisha? Of course we'll be there. But don't expect the entire village to come to greet you.' I chuckled, assuming he was just teasing me, but nothing could have prepared me for the scene that awaited me upon landing.

The airport was a sea of loud fans, eager followers and curious locals, all gathered to welcome me back. In the midst of the crowd, I spotted my father and sister, their faces beaming as they waved and shouted, 'Welcome, Manisha!' The sheer intensity of the reception took my breath away, and I dashed into my father's arms, tears of joy cascading down my cheeks. In that moment, I shared in my father's pride, as well as that of the entire village. The journey from the airport to Munger felt like a parade in my honour. My entire neighbourhood erupted in celebration, with people dancing, beating drums and showering me with flowers. Every street, rooftop and tree branch was lined with eager faces, all thrilled to catch a glimpse of their local star. Upon reaching our home, I quickly realized that my visit would be anything but a peaceful retreat.

Each day brought a steady stream of visitors, all seeking autographs, sharing stories and requesting interviews. Local YouTube channels wanted to produce content featuring me, while aspiring dancers approached me with hopes that I could help them towards success. Even after a week, the crowds showed no signs of thinning. I was deeply touched by all the love I was given but was also very aware my new status as a symbol of hope and success for my community.

During my time in Munger, I took a trip to Jamalpur to visit my mother, Sarika accompanying me as always. The moment I saw my mother, I couldn't hold back my tears of happiness and wrapped my arms around her. Over the next couple of days, I eagerly related my experiences from *Bigg Boss* to her, shared every detail of my music video collaboration with Tony Kakkar and celebrated my achievements. My mother listened, her eyes full of pride, and she offered me invaluable advice. 'Always show kindness to those who stood by you in your darkest days,' she counselled, 'and remember to stay honest and humble, regardless of how far you go.' I assured her that I would remain grounded and continue to help those in need. This conversation was very significant for me, for it prompted deep reflection. I reaffirmed the promise I had made to myself during my last visit: to never lose hope and to always have faith in myself.

Jhalak Dikhhla Jaa

My journey in Munger concluded, and I made my way back to Mumbai. Soon, I received an unexpected phone call that would change everything. It was an invitation to participate as a wild card contestant on the renowned dance show *Jhalak Dikhhla Jaa*. This could significantly elevate my career, but I was also acutely aware that this was a formidable test. The demanding schedule and fierce competition were sure to push me to my limits, both physically and mentally.

Soon after I began the rigorous training for *Jhalak Dikhhla Jaa*, the toll it took on my body and mind quickly became evident. The extended hours of rehearsal drained my energy, and before long, I found myself grappling with multiple health problems. The intensity of the sessions triggered severe migraines that each demanding practice seemed to amplify. I also suffered from dehydration, which necessitated two trips to the hospital; a subsequent episode of food poisoning only added to my deteriorating condition.

Never Stop, Step Ahead

Even in the face of such physical suffering, I remained resolute. I turned again to my history, thinking about the many hurdles I had surmounted to arrive at this moment. When an injury loomed, I refused to let it derail my ambitions; instead, I decided to push forward. I was competing against experienced dancers, and there were times when I dealt with insecurities, wondering whether I truly belonged on the same stage as such accomplished artists. However, as the weeks progressed, my confidence and composure blossomed. My distinctive style and vibrant energy began to appeal to both the judges and the audience, and my initial doubts disappeared: I belonged there.

As the competition progressed, I stayed in it, moving to the later stages. Reaching the grand finale felt like a fantasy come to life. Standing on that stage, ready for my final performance, I took a moment to think about how far I had come—from the humble streets of Munger to the dazzling realm of Mumbai's entertainment scene.

When the results were finally revealed and my name echoed as the winner of *Jhalak Dikhhla Jaa*'s eleventh season, I was momentarily speechless. The idea of a wild card contestant outshining seasoned veterans was unfathomable. I was overwhelmed with emotion, and tears of joy poured down my cheeks. This victory was more than just a personal achievement; it represented every challenge I had faced and overcome, and every moment of uncertainty I had experienced. I had demonstrated to myself and to the world that with relentless, determined effort, even the wildest dreams can materialize.

As I stood there, drinking in the cheers and admiration from the audience, I knew that this was merely the beginning of my journey. My transformation from a small-town girl with grand aspirations to a nationally celebrated star testified to the importance of believing in oneself. Now, I set my sights on new horizons: the world of acting beckoned. Yet, no matter where my career took me, I knew I would always carry with me the lessons from the early parts of my remarkable journey. I clung to my mantra—'*Picture abhi baaki hai mere dost*' (The movie isn't over yet, my friend)—to remind myself that every ending was just a new beginning, and the best was yet to come.

As I prepared to embrace the next chapter of my life, I thought back to my *Bigg Boss* audition tape, filled with the energy and charm that had become my trademark.

Hello, namaste, pranaam,
Bigg Boss *aur* Bigg Boss *ki aankh,*
Hum hain Manisha Rani,
Hamari mast hai kahani,
Hum Bihar ke ek chhote se town ki hasina,
Aur jisko dekh ke acche acche logon ke nikal jaata hai pasina,
Jo bhi samajhta hai humko halwa,
Achha baad mein dikhata hai apna jalwa,
Tab beta log chaate rah jaata hai mera talwa,
Ab dekhiye hum hain bilkul kamaal,
If you will select me for *Bigg Boss* Season 16,
Toh pehle hi bata dete hain ki aapke season mein hoga dhamaal,
Acting dance drama comedy ko kiye bina na aaye mujhe chain,

Munger ki Rani

Ye sab na kare to ho jaaye bechain,
Jaisi bhi hain, han khud ki hain bahut badi fan,
One piece hain poore world mein hai dekhiye hum tattoo bhi karwaaye hain, I love myself,
Ab aap hamein poochhenge ki hum karte kya hai?
I am a social media influencer and a super one-of-a-kind entertainer,
Aur haan part time mein apna adao sa ladka logon ko pagal karte hai,
Aur Bigg Boss *mein aana mera sapna hai kyun ki hum laakhon dilon ki dhadkan banna chahte hai,*
Sab ke dilon pe raaj karna chahte hai,
Sab ki favourite banana chahte hain,
Aur Bigg Boss *show mere liye ekdum perfect hai,*
Kyon ki Bigg Boss *mein real personality ko dikhaya jata hai,*
Aur hum real mein itni mast hai ki hum ko kuch karne ka zaroorat hi nahi padega,
Hum jo likh denge woh script ho jaega,
Jo bol denge woh dialogue ho jaega,
Jo kar denge woh kamal ho jaega,
Aur isi tarah se aapka Bigg Boss Season 16 *ekdum dhamaal ho jaega!*

These words, filled with energy and optimism, marked the beginning of an extraordinary adventure. With every obstacle I faced and every victory I achieved, I would keep crafting my own narrative—one woven with aspirations, resilience and the unyielding spirit of a girl from Bihar who bravely aspired to touch the stars.

My story is far from over, and I have many more chapters to write. But even in those years, it was certain to me that dance would always be at the heart of my journey and always guide me toward new horizons.

Acknowledgements

Writing a book is never a solitary act. It is built on the shoulders of those who walk beside us, support us and believe in us—even when we falter.

To my father, Brij Bhushan Sawhney—thank you for your unwavering support, quiet strength and belief in my dreams.

To my brother who has also been a father figure to me, Aneesh Dev (Bhaiya)—my guiding light and constant source of clarity. Your presence in my life has been both grounding and inspiring.

To Riti Chopra—thank you for the years we shared and for your continued kindness and encouragement.

To my mentor, Ekta Kapoor (Ma'am)—thank you for your guidance, trust and for showing me what it means to lead with courage and imagination.

To Farah Khan (Di)—your guidance felt like family. You've been a sister when I needed one most.

To Siddharth Kumar Tewary (Dada), who held my hand and lifted me up when I was at my lowest, giving me the strength and the reboot I needed.

Acknowledgements

To my lifelines Shabir Ahluwalia, Kanchi Kaul, Tanusri Dasgupta, Gayatri Gill and my dearest Verun Baabar, Shivngi Baabar, Rohini Vakil Kapoor and Vishal Singh—thank you for your friendship, faith and for always showing up.

To Prakash Paswan, more a younger brother than house help—thank you for more than a decade of unwavering support, for staying by my side through every rise and fall and for always cheering me on.

To Chitresh Soni—for your steady guidance and unwavering support throughout this journey.

To my literary agent and guide, Ms. Lipika Bhushan—thank you for championing this book with insight, passion and a steady hand.

To Tusharika Sharma, my associate writer—your dedication, energy and creativity have been invaluable.

To my editor, Anshu Dogra—thank you for your thoughtful direction and sharp editorial eye.

To Gurveen Chadha and her brilliant editing team at Penguin Random House India—your commitment and care have made this book stronger in every way.

Above all, my heartfelt gratitude to Manisha Rani for placing her trust in me and allowing me the honour of telling her life story.

And to you, the reader—thank you for allowing these words into your life. May you find something here that stays with you.

With heartfelt gratitude,
Sakett Saawhney

Scan QR code to access the
Penguin Random House India website

Praise for the Forge & Fracture series:

'**Glorious** (and very stabby!) ... a heroine you instantly root for and admire.'
The New York Times

'A fresh take on faerie magic.'
Leigh Bardugo

'Vividly expressive, riotously queer, beautifully Black and wildly creative ... **a pleasure to read**. If this is what she can do as a debut, there's no stopping her.'
Locus Magazine

'Nothing short of **a spectacular debut** ... a groundbreaking addition to the fantasy genre.'
Ayana Gray

'An addicting, original story. **Will delight readers of all ages**.'
Booklist

'Every sentence will thunder through your bones.'
Roshani Chokshi

'A **thrilling** read you won't want to put down.'
The Scotsman

'**Wildly imaginative** and refreshingly diverse.'
J. Elle

'Will pull readers in.'
Kirkus Reviews

'**An intricate, historically rich tapestry.**
Fans of Holly Black and Sarah J. Maas will love this.'
School Library Journal

'**I couldn't stop reading** it,
and when I finished all I wanted was more.'
Daniel José Older

'Fast-paced ... **a fresh take** on inclusive historical fantasy.'
NPR

'**A richly woven fantasy** ... a clever, entertaining, thoughtful read.'
Shelf Awareness

'An **absolute feast** of imagination.
Complex, brooding, impossible to put down.'
Scott Reintgen

'Combining Yoruba myths, Shakespearean drama, a love triangle,
and a race-against time adventure, this fantasy debut
certainly **packs a punch**.'
Irish Examiner

'Williams's **fast-paced adventure** gallops apace ... once
immersed in the world of Joan Sands, you're not going to want to leave.'
Tor.com

'A fun, quick read with diverse and queer characters
a reader will happily follow into battle.'
Historical Novel Society